MW00598271

CAMPAIGN 397

CAPE MATAPAN 1941

Cunningham's Mediterranean Triumph

ANGUS KONSTAM

ILLUSTRATED BY ADAM TOOBY

Series editor Nikolai Bogdanovic

OSPREY PUBLISHING
Bloomsbury Publishing Plc
Kemp House, Chawley Park, Cumnor Hill, Oxford OX2 9PH, UK
29 Earlsfort Terrace, Dublin 2, Ireland
1385 Broadway, 5th Floor, New York, NY 10018, USA
E-mail: info@ospreypublishing.com
www.ospreypublishing.com

OSPREY is a trademark of Osprey Publishing Ltd

First published in Great Britain in 2023

© Osprey Publishing Ltd, 2023

All rights reserved. No part of this publication may be reproduced or
transmitted in any form or by any means, electronic or mechanical,
including photocopying, recording, or any information storage or retrieval
system, without prior permission in writing from the publishers.

A catalogue record for this book is available from the British Library.

ISBN: PB 9781472857231; eBook 9781472857248; ePDF 9781472857255;
XML 9781472857262

23 24 25 26 27 10 9 8 7 6 5 4 3 2 1

Maps by Bounford.com
3D BEVs by Paul Kime
Index by Sharon Redmayne
Typeset by PDQ Digital Media Solutions, Bungay, UK
Printed and bound in India by Replika Press Private Ltd.
Osprey Publishing supports the Woodland Trust, the UK's leading woodland
conservation charity.

Artist's note

Readers can find out more about the work of battlescene illustrator Adam
Tooby by visiting the following website:

www.adamtooby.com

To find out more about our authors and books visit
www.ospreypublishing.com. Here you will find extracts, author
interviews, details of forthcoming events and the option to sign up for
our newsletter.

Photographs

Unless otherwise indicated, the photographs that appear in this work are
from the Stratford Archive.

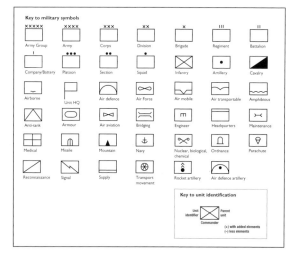

Front cover main illustration: Admiral Cattaneo's cruisers are
ambushed by Admiral Cunningham's battle fleet at 2230hrs on 28
March. (Adam Tooby)
Title page photograph: Cattaneo's cruisers steam westwards
through the Ionian Sea, with Cattaneo's flagship *Zara* in the lead.

CONTENTS

Operation *Gaudo* – the Cape Matapan operation

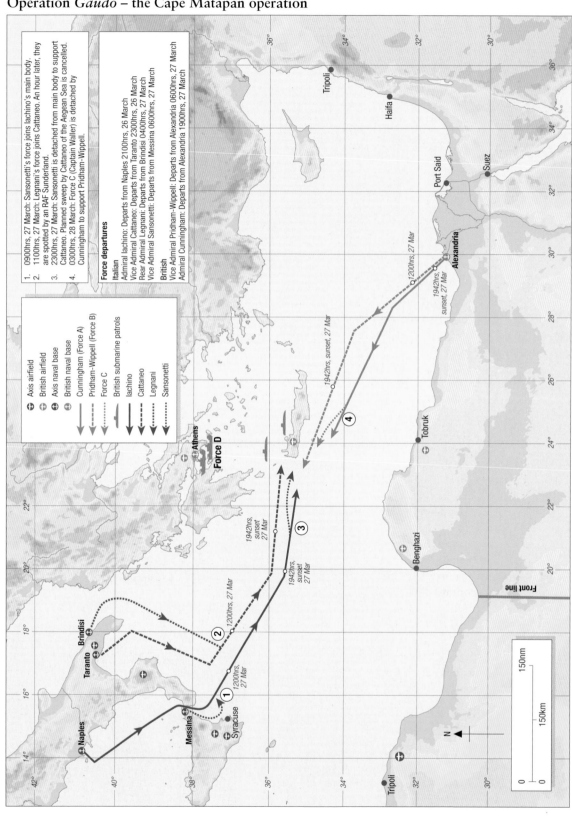

1. 0900hrs, 27 March: Sansonetti's force joins Iachino's main body.
2. 1100hrs, 27 March: Legnani's force joins Cattaneo. An hour later, they are spotted by an RAF Sunderland.
3. 2300hrs, 27 March: Sansonetti is detached from main body to support Cattaneo. Planned sweep by Cattaneo of the Aegean Sea is cancelled.
4. 0300hrs, 28 March: Force C (Captain Waller) is detached by Cunningham to support Pridham-Wippell.

Force departures

Italian
Admiral Iachino: Departs from Naples 2100hrs, 26 March
Vice Admiral Cattaneo: Departs from Taranto 2300hrs, 26 March
Rear Admiral Legnani: Departs from Brindisi 0400hrs, 27 March
Vice Admiral Sansonetti: Departs from Messina 0600hrs, 27 March

British
Vice Admiral Pridham-Wippell: Departs from Alexandria 0600hrs, 27 March
Admiral Cunningham: Departs from Alexandria 1900hrs, 27 March

Axis airfield
British airfield
Axis naval base
British naval base
Cunningham (Force A)
Pridham-Wippell (Force B)
Force C
British submarine patrols
Iachino
Cattaneo
Legnani
Sansonetti

INTRODUCTION

The Battle of Cape Matapan, fought off the southern coast of Greece in late March 1941, was a mixture of the old and the new. It was an unusual naval engagement, as it was more of a running fight than a classic sea battle. However, the whole battle centred on the presence of battleships – most notably the flagships of the two rival commanders, admirals Cunningham and Iachino. Its climax came when Cunningham's three battleships ambushed the enemy in a night action, with utterly devastating consequences. In this respect Matapan was decided in the age-old way, using naval firepower to deliver a result. For the British, their Mediterranean battle fleet was very much in the right place at the right time. This, though, was only achieved by the use of three far more modern tools.

The first was naval intelligence, acquired through the breaking of Italian naval signal codes. This was coupled with the impressive use of misinformation – convincing Axis spies that the British battle fleet was safely in port, rather than at sea, and within striking range of the Italians. As a result, when the battle began, Admiral Iachino had no idea his British counterpart was nearby. The second modern aspect was naval airpower. While both sides made use of aerial reconnaissance, the inclusion of a British carrier in Cunningham's battle fleet gave him a marked edge. As a result, as the battle progressed, Cunningham usually had a shrewd idea where Iachino was, while the Italian commander remained largely in the dark.

Then, when contact was made, the British carrier *Formidable* launched a series of air strikes on the Italian flagship, and crippled her. This turned the running battle into a pursuit, as Cunningham desperately tried to bring her to bay before nightfall. This aggressive use of naval air strikes set up the conditions which led to the decisive night action that followed. This night engagement still needed another modern element to make it happen. In March 1941, the Royal Navy had an early form of radar fitted to some of its warships, while the system was still unknown to the Italian Regia Marina. At Matapan, the surface-search radar fitted to the battleship *Valiant* helped Cunningham guide his battle fleet into the perfect position to ambush the

Radar gave Cunningham's fleet a real edge at Matapan. The battleship *Valiant*, the carrier *Formidable* and the cruiser *Ajax* all carried a Type 279 radar set, first introduced in 1940, which although primarily an air-warning radar, had a secondary surface-search capability. The information was collated in a radar plot room such as this.

The Italian heavy cruisers of Sansonetti's division pictured in action during the Battle of Calabria in June 1940. Although fast, elegant warships, they were lightly protected, and therefore as vulnerable to enemy fire as their lighter British opponents.

enemy. This gave his fleet a crucial advantage, and Cunningham used it to great effect to deliver his crushing blow.

Above all, though, the Royal Navy's dramatic victory at Matapan came about thanks to one man. Admiral Cunningham, commander of the British Mediterranean Fleet, had many virtues, including a gift for cool decision-making, meticulous planning and an intuitive grasp of the nuances of modern naval warfare. He was also one of the most aggressive naval commanders of the war, willing to flout tactical orthodoxy in order to defeat the enemy. Like Nelson before him (a commander to whom Cunningham was often compared), he regarded the enemy as someone to be defeated, in as decisive a manner as possible. Like Nelson, Cunningham was regarded as a lucky commander. Cunningham, though, a consummate naval professional, made sure that he created his own luck.

ORIGINS OF THE CAMPAIGN

In the opening months of 1941 it appeared that the British were in the ascendancy in the Mediterranean. In the Western Desert General Archibald Wavell's Army of the Nile had pushed the Italians out of Cyrenaica, and had reached El Agheila on the Gulf of Sidra, barely 300 miles from Tripoli. There Wavell's army paused to regroup and resupply before continuing its advance. During the previous year there were two significant encounters between the British and Italian navies, at Calabria (or Punta Stilo) in July and Cape Spartivento (or Teulada) in November. On both occasions the Italian fleet had broken off the fight, ceding the sea to the Royal Navy. That November the

British cruisers in action during the indecisive Battle of Cape Spartivento, fought in November 1940. This was the last large-scale sortie of the Italian battle fleet before the Matapan operation, and the lack of aggression shown then was taken by the British as a sign of weakness. In fact, it was largely the result of political interference in Italian naval operations.

Fleet Air Arm also attacked the Italian naval base at Taranto and crippled the Italian battle fleet, putting it out of action for several months.

Meanwhile, in the Central Mediterranean the fortress island of Malta continued to be a thorn in the enemy's side, as it sat astride the Axis convoy routes to North Africa. It became a useful base from which to harry Italian supply convoys running between Italy and its North African colony of Libya. The effective neutralizing of the Italian battle fleet also allowed the British to run its own supply and reinforcement convoys from Gibraltar to Malta, and on to Alexandria. By year's end, for the first time since Italy entered the war, it looked like the British position in the Mediterranean not only looked stable, but was improving. However, change was literally in the air.

The Italian fascist leader Benito Mussolini, inspecting the crew of the battleship *Littorio*, a sister ship of the *Vittorio Veneto*. During the war he constantly micro-managed the operations of the Regia Marina, and was politically unwilling to oppose the strategic wishes of his German allies.

On 10 January the aircraft carrier *Illustrious*, which had launched the Taranto raid, was bombed as she passed through the Sicilian Narrows, between Sicily and Tunisia. Her assailants were a mixture of Italian torpedo-bombers and two squadrons of German Ju 87 Stuka dive-bombers. The carrier was badly damaged, but managed to reach Malta, where temporary repairs were carried out. She then continued on to Alexandria, and ultimately to the United States, to be repaired. This, though, proved that the British Mediterranean Fleet now faced a new threat. The Stukas were from the Luftwaffe's Fliegerkorps X, an air armada of bombers and fighters which had just arrived in the Mediterranean theatre, and were based in Sicily. These German airmen had been specially trained in anti-shipping operations.

Meanwhile, the British offensive in North Africa ground to a halt, as Wavell was at the limits of his lines of communications. It would take time to bring up supplies to allow him to resume the offensive. Even here, though, change was afoot. In February the first German reinforcements arrived in Tripoli – the advanced guard of General Erwin Rommell's Afrika Korps. However, at the same time as the battered Italian troops in Libya were given a breathing space, other Italian forces were also encountering unexpected resistance elsewhere. In late 1940 Mussolini launched an unprovoked invasion of Greece. The springboard for his invasion was Albania, which had been overrun and annexed by Italy in April of the previous year. Despite being outnumbered, the Greeks fought stubbornly, making good use of the rugged terrain in the area. Eventually, over the winter, they pushed the Italians back into Albania.

While this was a humiliating setback for Mussolini, it also worried Hitler too. He was planning to invade the Soviet Union the following summer, and wanted his southern flank to be secure. So, he decided to intervene in the theatre. The arrival of Fliegerkorps X was a precursor to a much larger German military commitment. This involved a German invasion of the Balkans, which comprised a rapid advance through Yugoslavia, followed by a descent on Greece from the north. When word of these plans reached Whitehall, Churchill, promised the Greek government that he would send military help. This decision was made without any real consultation with the Imperial General Staff, who disapproved, because it meant delaying the renewal of Wavell's offensive in Libya. Instead, a major portion of Wavell's Army of the Nile would now be diverted to Greece.

The movement of these Commonwealth troops to Greece was codenamed Operation *Lustre*. From 5 March onwards, a series of transport convoys were sent from Egypt to Piraeus near Athens. This operation was conducted successfully, thanks largely to the protection offered to the transports by Admiral Cunningham's Mediterranean Fleet. After shipping the convoy of troops to Greece, Operation *Lustre* turned into a resupply operation. By then, though, the presence of Fliegerkorps X in Sicily had effectively severed sea communications through the Mediterranean between Gibraltar, Malta and Alexandria. So, shipping was sent to Egypt by the longer but considerably safer route around the southern tip of Africa and up the Suez Canal. Operation *Lustre* merely extended this already lengthy line of supply and communication by another 500 miles.

Throughout March the Mediterranean Fleet continued to protect the *Lustre* convoys, operating between Alexandria and Piraeus, and maintaining sea communications with Malta. Cunningham had become concerned about the increased activity of the Luftwaffe, though, which included the dropping of magnetic mines in the Suez Canal. The canal was both the lifeline of the Mediterranean Fleet, and of the Commonwealth troops in North Africa. One of the results of this aerial mining, carried out by aircraft operating from Libya, was to delay the arrival of the aircraft carrier *Formidable*. She had been sent to Alexandria to replace *Illustrious*, and this delay was exacerbated by her being used to support operations in Italian Somaliland, on the shores of the Red Sea. So, her arrival in Alexandria on 10 March was a relief to Cunningham, as it markedly increased his fleet's capabilities.

This was particularly timely, as the Italian Naval Command, the Supermarina, was now being pressured by its German allies to do something to stem the tide of supplies flowing into Greece. Eventually, on Mussolini's insistence, the Italian fleet commander Admiral Angelo Iachino, then based in Naples, was ordered to take steps to interdict the *Lustre* convoys. This would set in train the events that would lead to the Battle of Matapan. By then the British intelligence gatherers in Bletchley Park had broken the Enigma codes used by both the Italian navy and by the Luftwaffe. So, relevant signal intercepts were passed on to the British Admiralty, and from there they were forwarded to Cunningham's flagship *Warspite*. That meant that by 25 March, Cunningham knew that Iachino was planning to put to sea.

Cunningham's first task was to protect the *Lustre* convoys. So, on

The landing of Commonwwealth troops in Piraeus, the port serving Athens, in early March 1941. Operation *Lustre*, the transport of British and Commonwealth troops to Greece, served as the catalyst for the Italian naval sortie that led to the battle of Cape Matapan.

26 May the departure of convoy GA-8 of a single unladen merchant ship in Piraeus was delayed 'due to logistical problems', while the northbound convoy AG-9, which was already at sea, was quietly turned about, and ordered to loiter to the north of the Egyptian coast. These excuses and diversions were necessary, because the Axis were unaware that their Enigma codes had been broken. So, rather than reveal this, other excuses had to be found to explain the chain of events which Cunningham would instigate to counter Iachino's sortie.

The Italian Supermarina, or Naval High Command, was under intense pressure from the Germans to conduct a sortie to harass the *Lustre* convoys between Egypt and Greece. The Italian navy's senior officers (on the left), led by Admiral Riccardi, meet their German naval counterparts during a conference in Merano in February, in the initial planning phase of the operation.

There were other signs that the Italian fleet was about to come out. First, there was an increase in the number of Axis reconnaissance flights over southern Greece, the Aegean, Crete and the Ionian Sea. This incuded regular reconnaissance sorties over Alexandria by aircraft flying from Rhodes, several of which were intercepted by British fighters. Secondly, regular signals traffic increased between Rome and the naval bases at Naples, Taranto and Brindisi, and the Italian air force bases in southern Italy, Albania and Rhodes. Sure enough, late on 26 March the various elements of the Italian fleet put to sea from several ports, and proceeded to a series of arranged rendezvous points in the Ionian Sea.

Iachino, in his flagship, the battleship *Vittorio Veneto*, sailed from Naples at 2100hrs that evening, accompanied by a flotilla of destroyers. By dawn the force had passed through the Straits of Messina, and at 0900hrs on 27 March it rendezvoused with the 3rd Cruiser Division, and its own destroyer escort, which had sailed from Messina at 0615hrs. It then steamed east. At 2300hrs that evening the 1st Cruiser Division and its destroyer escort left Taranto, and at 1100hrs it was joined at sea by the 8th Cruiser Division, which had sailed from Brindisi shortly before dawn. By then, Cunningham had learned of these naval movements, and was preparing his own response. To maintain the cover for Enigma, an RAF Sunderland flying boat was in place at 1220hrs on 27 March to sight Iachino's main force, 100 miles east of the Sicilian coast. In fact it only spotted Admiral Luigi Sansonetti's cruisers.

Just over six hours before, Cunningham's deputy Vice Admiral Henry Pridham-Wippell put to sea. His four light cruisers and escorting destroyers would be in position to the south-west of Crete by dawn the following day. Cunningham also planned to follow with his battle fleet, but for now he was happy to maintain the illusion that no sailing was planned. Dinner invitations were sent out from *Warspite*, suggesting she would remain in harbour all evening. Then, that afternoon, Cunningham went ashore to play golf with the Japanese consul. An aide accompanied him with a suitcase, suggesting the admiral would spend the night ashore at his residency. There is no record of how Cunningham fared on the course, but he was a keen golfer. Afterwards he retured to his residency, and then slipped away in time for the fleet's departure at 1900hrs. So, that evening, various Italian and British naval groups were busily converging on each other, all heading towards the same patch of water to the south-west of Crete.

CHRONOLOGY

26 March 1941

0900hrs	The Italian fleet prepares for a sortie as far as the western coast of Crete.
1030hrs	Cunningham is informed of the operation by the Admiralty.
1400hrs	Operation *Lustre* convoys between Alexandria and Piraeus are rescheduled.

27 March 1941

0600hrs	Force B sails from Alexandria, to cruise off south-west Crete.
1200hrs	The Italian fleet is sighted by RAF search aircraft in the Ionian Sea.
1400hrs	In Alexandria, Cunningham goes ashore to play golf.
1900hrs	The British battle fleet sails from Alexandria.

28 March 1941

0628hrs	A search plane from the *Vittorio Veneto* locates Pridham-Wippell's cruisers.
0720hrs	At sunrise, British aircraft from *Formidable* locate the Italian Force Z.
0729hrs	Another aircraft from *Formidable* locates Force X.
0745hrs	British cruisers sight Force X.
0820hrs	Sansonetti's Force X opens fire on Pridham-Wippell's cruisers.
0829hrs	*Gloucester* returns fire.
0851hrs	Cunningham detaches *Valiant* from the battle fleet to support Pridham-Wippell.
0854hrs	An aircraft from *Formidable* sights the Italian battleship near Gavdos.
0855hrs	Sansonetti ceases fire and withdraws to the north-west.
0917hrs	Cattaneo's Force Z alters course towards the Calabrian coast.
1058–1127hrs	Action between the *Vittorio Veneto* and British cruisers.
1127hrs	*Formidable*'s first air strike against the *Vittorio Veneto*. Iachino withdraws towards the north-west.
1205hrs	Air attack on Force X by Swordfish flying from Crete.
1230hrs	A second air strike is launched from *Formidable*. Pridham-Wippell's force rejoins the battle fleet.

1420–1450hrs   Unsuccessful air attack on the *Vittorio Veneto* by RAF Blenheims, operating from Greece.

1510–1525hrs   Second air strike from *Formidable* on the *Vittorio Veneto*. The battleship is hit by a torpedo.

1515–1645hrs   Unsuccessful air attacks on Cattaneo's cruisers by RAF Blenheims.

1520–1700hrs   Unsuccessful air attacks on Sansonetti's cruisers by RAF Blenheims.

1558hrs   A shadowing Albacore reports the Italian flagship is operating at reduced speed.

1644hrs   Cunningham orders Pridham-Wippell to regain contact with Italian fleet.

1700hrs   Iachino orders his cruiser groups to concentrate around the fleet flagship.

1720hrs   *Vittorio Veneto* is now capable of making only 16 knots.

1735hrs   *Formidable* launches the third air strike.

1831hrs   *Walrus*' Swordfish floatplane resumes shadowing the Italian fleet.

1918hrs   *Orion* sights the Italian fleet at a range of 10 miles.

1925hrs   Air attack on the Italian cruisers by aircraft from *Formidable*. *Pola* is badly damaged.

1945hrs   *Pola* drops out of the Italian formation.

1949hrs   Pridham-Wippell reduces speed to decrease his ships' visibility.

2015hrs   *Orion* detects enemy ships on her radar.

2018hrs   Cattaneo is ordered to turn back with *Zara* and *Fiume*, to assist *Pola*.

2038hrs   Cunningham orders his destroyers to attack the enemy battle fleet.

2048hrs   *Vittorio Veneto* alters course to the north-west.

2145hrs   *Ajax* detects the enemy on her radar.

2202hrs   Pridham-Wippell turns away to the north.

2203hrs   *Valiant* detects a stationary enemy ship on her radar.

2210hrs   *Valiant* sights a warship 6 miles away. Cunningham alters course towards the contact.

2220hrs   The ship detected by *Valiant* is at 4½ miles.

2223hrs   The destroyer *Stuart* sights the line of enemy ships.

2224hrs   The British battle fleet turns onto a parallel course, and is ordered to open fire at a range of 2 miles.

2225hrs   *Formidable* is ordered out of the line and alters course to the north.

2227hrs	The destroyer *Greyhound* illuminates the enemy cruisers with her searchlight.
2231hrs	Fire is switched to the Italian destroyers, which attempt a torpedo attack.
2238hrs	The British destroyers are ordered to finish off the enemy cruisers.
2243hrs	A flare fired by the *Vittorio Veneto* is spotted by *Orion* and *Gloucester*.
2252hrs	Pridham-Wippell alters course towards the Italian battleship.
2315hrs	The cruiser *Fiume* and destroyer *Alfieri* sink, and *Carducci* is engaged.
2317hrs	*Stuart* engages *Zara*, and an Italian destroyer.
2320hrs	The remaining Italian destroyers break contact.
2330hrs	*Carducci* sinks.
2332hrs	Cunningham orders any forces not engaged to withdraw to the north-east, including Pridham-Wippell.

29 March 1941

0140hrs	*Greyhound* and *Griffin* encounter the crippled *Pola*.
0220hrs	*Jervis* rescues survivors from *Zara*.
0240hrs	*Jervis* torpedoes *Zara*.
0246hrs	*Zara* sinks.
0325hrs	Survivors are rescued from *Pola*.
0340hrs	*Jervis* and *Nubian* torpedo *Pola*.
0403hrs	*Pola* sinks.
1530hrs	*Formidable* is attacked by German bombers.
1630hrs	Iachino's fleet enters Taranto.

30 March 1941

| 1730hrs | Cunningham's fleet enters Alexandria. |

A Swordfish on a reconnaissance mission is launched from *Formidable* in the Eastern Mediterranean. Accompanying her is Admiral. Cunningham's flagship *Warspite*. The photograph was taken from the *Valiant* during an operation just days before the Battle of Matapan.

OPPOSING COMMANDERS

REGIA MARINA

Acting Admiral (Ammiraglio d'Armata) Angelo Iachino (1889–1976), the son of a schoolteacher, was from Liguria in north-western Italy. He joined the navy in 1904, and by the time Italy entered World War I, he was a lieutenant (*Tenente*) serving aboard the battleship *Giulio Cesare*. In 1917 he was given command of a torpedo boat operating in the Adriatic, and saw action off Pola. During the 1920s Iachino commanded a gunboat in Chinese waters. Later, he was given command of a destroyer, and then, after promotion to captain (*Capitano di Vascello*), the command of the cruiser *Armando Diaz*. By 1938 he had risen to flag rank as a rear admiral (*Ammiraglio di Divisione*), and commanded Italian naval forces during their intervention in the Spanish Civil War, and again during the Abyssinian crisis. In 1939 Iachino became a vice admiral (*Ammiraglio di Squadra*), and when Italy entered the war in June 1940, he was given command of the powerful 2nd Naval Squadron. He participated in the Battle of Cape Spartiavento in November 1940, and afterwards he replaced the battle fleet commander Admiral Inigo Campioni.

Iachino was hampered by the damage inflicted on the battle fleet at Taranto, which meant that for the Matapan operation only one battleship was available to him. Although a skilled naval commander, Iachino had been

Admiral Angelo Iachino (left), Commander-in-Chief of the Italian fleet, pictured on the bridge of his flagship. A gifted and cerebral commander, he only made one poor decision during the battle, but it proved a costly one.

Vice Admiral Carlo Cattaneo was an experienced cruiser commander, who had proved his worth in action the previous year. At Matapan he felt his evening mission to rescue the *Pola* was foolhardy, but was ordered to carry it through. It cost him his life.

impeded by restrictive orders from his risk-averse superiors in the Supermarina (the Italian Naval High Command), who made it plain that Italy's only fully operational battleship was not to be placed in jeopardy. At Matapan Iachino never really made a mistake during the battle, until he ordered his subordinate Vice Admiral Cattaneo to return to the east, to look for the crippled cruiser *Pola*. However, not only had Iachino suffered from a lack of reliable intelligence that day, but the air support he had been offered never materialized. So, his decision to release Cattaneo was understandable, despite it having catastrophic results. This probably explains why Iachino remained in post after Matapan. He went on to perform well at the two battles of Sirte, but he was eventually replaced in early 1943. After the war Iachino wrote of his wartime career, devoting a lot of time to countering criticism of his performance at Matapan.

The naval commander whom Iachino ordered to search for the *Pola* was **Vice Admiral Carlo Cattaneo** (1883–1941). A Neapolitan, Cattaneo joined the navy in 1902, and after his cadetship he served in the Italo-Turkish War (1911–12), distinguishing himself in command of a naval landing party. During World War I he commanded a torpedo boat, before serving in destroyers. In 1920 he was promoted to lieutenant-commander (*Capitano di Corvetta*), and served as Italy's naval attaché in Constantinople. Other similar staff duties followed, before his promotion to full captain in 1932, and with it the command of the cruiser *Di Giussano*. After that came promotion to flag rank, and in 1938 he became a vice admiral. At the outbreak of war he became commander of the 3rd Cruiser Division, and showed spirit during the Battle of Calabria – one of the few Italian flag officers to do so.

By early 1941 Cattaneo was given command of the prestigious 1st Cruiser Division, flying his flag in *Zara*. At Matapan he performed his duties well, but questioned his orders from Iachino to lead his whole force back to rescue the *Pola*. Cattaneo felt the task could be performed by more expendable destroyers, but he was overruled. Consequently, Cattaneo was killed during the opening moments of the night action, when *Zara*'s bridge was hit by a 15-inch shell. Afterwards, he was posthumously awarded a medal for valour. The other senior Italian commander at Matapan was **Vice Admiral Luigi Sansonetti** (1888–1959), who commanded the 3rd Cruiser Division. He joined the navy in 1905, and like Cattaneo he distinguished himself during landing operations in Tripoli during the Italo-Turkish War.

By 1914 he was a lieutenant, and served on the staff of the Italian battle squadron, before commanding a torpedo boat in the Adriatic. During the interwar years he was given command of destroyers, and eventually rose to command destroyer flotillas. He reached the rank of captain in 1932, and after various staff posts he was given command of the cruiser *Eugenio di Savoia* in 1935. By 1940 he commanded the 7th Cruiser Squadron, and led it into action at the

Battle of Calabria. That August he was given command of the 3rd Cruiser Division, flying his flag in the *Trieste*. At Matapan Sansonetti proved to be a cautious commander, showing reluctance to closely engage Pridham-Wippell's lighter cruisers, and withdrew when pressed. After Matapan Sansonetti was given shore appointments. Incidentally, his son, a lieutenant, was one of the few survivors of the destroyer *Alfieri* when she was sunk during the Matapan night action.

ROYAL NAVY

Admiral Andrew B. Cunningham (1883–1963), known as 'ABC' to his men, was born in Dublin, but educated at Edinburgh Academy. He joined the navy as a cadet in 1897, and subsequently saw action ashore during the Second Boer War (1899–1902). In World War I he served in torpedo boats and destroyers, and saw action again during the Dardanelles campaign. He ended the war as a commander. He headed destroyer flotillas during the 1920s, and gained his flag in 1932, when he was given command of the Mediterranean Fleet's destroyer flotillas. So, by 1939 he was regarded as a highly experienced 'Mediterranean hand'. He became a vice admiral in 1936, and served as the deputy to the fleet's commander, Admiral Dudley Pound, commanding the battlecruiser squadron. In June 1939, though, as an admiral, he was given command of the Mediterranean Fleet, a post he held until the spring of 1942.

Admiral Andrew B. Cunningham, Commander-in-Chief of the British Mediterranean Fleet. At Matapan he was determined to pursue and destroy the Italian fleet, and displayed the skill and aggression that earned him a place as one of the Royal Navy's greatest admirals.

Cunningham possessed great courage and a steely determination. He was highly aggressive in terms of tactics, but intelligent with it, and he had the ability to quickly grasp an operational situation, and act accordingly. He was also resolute when under pressure, yet flexible enough to react to changing events as the situation demanded. In short he was a commander who thought on his feet, but backed this up with an ability to plan in detail, and ensure his subordinates knew exactly what was expected of them. Many found him difficult, and he suffered neither fools nor 'yes men'. However, he was thoroughly professional, and expected excellence from both himself and those who served under him. 'ABC' was, almost certainly, the most gifted naval commander of the war. After Matapan he supervised the evacuation of Crete, when his determination ensured that the operation would continue, regardless of losses. He was made Admiral of the Fleet in 1943, and went on to oversee the Allied landings on Sicily and the Italian mainland, and the surrender of the Italian battle fleet. He subsequently served as First Sea Lord until he retired from the service in 1946. Cunningham was very much the right man for the job. It would be hard to think of anyone better qualified to command the Mediterranean Fleet in time of crisis.

OPPOSITE
Vice Admiral Luigi Sansonetti ordered the firing of the opening shots of the battle, when his cruisers engaged Vice Admiral Pridham-Wippell's force off Gavdos Island that morning. He wisely decided to break contact, though, as he felt he was being drawn into a trap.

Vice Admiral Henry Pridham-Wippell was Cunningham's deputy, and the Mediterranean Fleet's Vice Admiral of Light Forces (VALF). A skilled cruiser and destroyer commander, his task was to locate the enemy, and then to shadow him until he could be brought to battle.

Vice Admiral Henry Pridham-Wippell (1885–1952) was Cunningham's second-in-command during the Matapan operation, and bore the official title of Vice Admiral, Light Forces (which was abbreviated to VALF). Born in Kent and schooled in Greenwich, in 1900 he became a naval cadet at Dartmouth. By 1914 he was a lieutenant , and was serving aboard the battleship *Audacity* when she was sunk. He subsequently served in *Warspite*, and ended the war as a Lieutenant-Commander, and the commander of destroyers in Gallipoli and the Adriatic. After his promotion to captain in 1926 he was given command of the cruiser *Enterprise*, serving in the East Indies. He subsequently commanded both destroyer flotillas and cruisers, and was promoted to flag rank in 1938. When the war began, he had a desk job in the Admiralty, but he was soon given command of the 1st Battle Squadron, and that October became the commander of the Mediterranean Fleet's light forces. He was promoted to vice admiral in January 1941. Pridham-Wippell had been friends with Cunningham since they served on destroyers in the Dardanelles together, and both respected each other. Pridham-Wippell was thoroughly professional, but he also displayed both initiative and courage. He was the perfect deputy to 'ABC', as he could be relied upon to accurately second-guess Cunningham's thoughts, and act accordingly. Therefore, he enjoyed his superior's complete confidence.

OPPOSING FORCES

REGIA MARINA

The *Vittorio Veneto* was a thoroughly modern battleship, having only entered service just weeks before Italy joined the war. While other Italian battleships had been built before World War I, and had subsequently been modernized, the *Vittorio Veneto* and her two Littorio-class sister ships had all been designed and built during the 1930s, and so reflected the latest generation of capital ship design. The *Vittorio Veneto* was armed with 38.1cm/50 (15-inch) Model 1934 guns, which in theory had a greater maximum range that their British counterparts. These fired a 1,952lb (884.8kg) armour-piercing shell, with a range of up to 46,807 yards (42,800m), the equivalent of more than 23 miles. These were mounted in three triple turrets. Unfortunately for the Regia Marina, though, these had teething problems – the salvoes fired from these turrets were widely spaced, which reduced their effectiveness. This problem was overcome, but not before Matapan.

The battleship also carried an impressive secondary battery, and an extensive array of medium- and close-range anti-aircraft (AA) weapons. In this respect the *Vittorio Veneto* was much better served than her British rivals. At Matapan, though, her main guns never fired in anger. Instead, it was her AA battery of twelve 90mm, twenty 37mm and sixteen 20mm guns that were used against three British carrier-borne air strikes. Despite this huge volume of fire, though, they only managed to shoot down one plane. The *Vittorio Veneto* was also faster than the battleships of Cunningham's battle fleet, making 30 knots, a good 5 knots faster than the British flagship. In terms of armour the Littorio class was well served by a 28cm protective belt, with turret and barbette armour up to 35cm thick. This, though, compared unfavourably with the British Queen Elizabeth-class battleships, which had a belt of up to 33cm (13 inches). Her Pugliese system of anti-torpedo bulges provided adequate underwater protection, but

Italy's fascist government placed great stock in the strength of its navy, as shown in this propaganda poster from 1940. After the Taranto raid of November 1940, though, Mussolini was reluctant to place what remained of his battle fleet in unnecessary danger. However, German pressure forced him to approve Iachino's planned sweep into the Ionian Sea that spring.

Italian heavy cruisers pictured at their berths in the port of Taranto. At Matatapan the 8-inch guns mounted in the Italian cruisers were notably superior in range and hitting power to Pridham-Wippell's British light cruisers, but problems in accuracy and fire control lessened their effectiveness.

when hit, the *Vittorio Veneto* was struck around her propellers and rudders – an area which was even the Achilles heel of the much-vaunted *Bismarck*.

The Italian cruisers at Matapan – apart from the two Abruzzi-class ones which took no part in the fighting – were heavy cruisers, armed with 20.3cm/53 Model 1929 (8-inch) guns. The two Trentos, though, carried the earlier 20.3cm/50 Model 1924 version. The guns were the same – only the mountings differed. All were mounted in four twin turrets, and fired a 276.2lb (125.3kg) armour-piercing shell, with a maximum range of 34,521 yards (31,566m). This was significantly longer than the 6-inch guns of the British light cruisers at Matapan, but accuracy was reduced by the poor quality of the rangefinders fitted to these Italian cruisers. The exception was the *Bolzano*, which had a more modern fire-control system. These cruisers also carried torpedoes, and an extensive AA battery of sixteen 100mm and four to six 40mm AA guns, as well as up to eight AA machine guns. Again, though, these lacked an effective overall AA fire-control system.

Although the Italian cruisers were all built over an eight-year period between 1925 and 1933, each group – the two Trentos, the three Zaras and the *Bolzano* – all varied slightly in terms of protection. Initially, their design emphasized speed over protection, and the Trentos only carried a 7cm belt of protective armour in a 'box citadel' system which only protected the ship's vitals – her propulsion system and magazines. This was increased to 15cm in the Zaras, although this meant a drop in speed from 36 to 32 knots. The *Bolzano* marked a retun to the Trento design, with minimal protection and maximum speed. At Matapan, though, this edge in speed allowed Vice Admiral Sansonetti's cruisers to close the range on their British opponents, and later to race away to safety.

Any cruiser armour, though, was not entirely proof against a torpedo hit, and *Pola* was unfortunate to be struck where the damage to her propulsion system was particularly effective. Also, no cruiser armour was proof against a 15-inch shell striking at a velocity of over 2,000 feet per second. That, ultimately, was a threat no Italian ship designer could ever have foreseen. During the night action at Matapan, the Italians suffered from not having radar – a technological advantage of which they were largely unaware.

The disaster at Matapan might have been averted by better training in night fighting, including the ability to visually detect the enemy in darkness. This, though, reflects one of the cardinal differences between the two sides. At Matapan the British were better trained in fighting night actions, and their lookouts were able to detect enemy ships in the dark while they themselves remained unseen. The Regia Marina had simply not developed night-fighting techniques adequately enough before the battle, while in the British Mediterranean Fleet this had been a priority. At Matapan a similar dearth of training manifested itself in two other ways. First, when attacked by *Formidable*'s air strike, the Italian fleet fired its AA guns almost indiscriminately – a criticism first levelled at it during the air raid on Taranto the previous November. According to some British airmen, the Italians even hit their own ships in their enthusiasm to blaze away.

Then, in both the *Vittorio Veneto* and the *Pola*, after being hit by a torpedo, both ships should have concentrated on isolating any flooding, and then restoring their ship's ability to get moving again. In the *Vittorio Veneto* Iachino reported that damage control was less efficient than it could have been, and so repairs to the ship's propulsion system took much longer than they should have. In *Pola* it was even worse. By the time the British found the ship, immobilized and drifting, most of her crew had already abandoned ship. Those who remained, according to the crew of the British destroyers who rescued them, were drunk. This suggests a failure of command aboard the ship, and a breakdown in morale. This in turn was probably the result of inadequate training. In the wartime Royal Navy, the need to save your own ship was intuitive, after extensive training in damage control – primarily the fight against flooding and fire, and the restoration of the ship's systems. In the Regia Marina at Matapan, this does not seem to have been the case, and so one good ship was placed at risk, and another lost.

The elegant heavy cruiser *Zara*, namesake of her four-ship class, and flagship of Vice Admiral Cattaneo. Although these ships were markedly better protected than the cruisers of the preceding Trento class, this was achieved by sacrificing some of their speed.

Many of the warships of Britain's Mediterranean Fleet were elderly, but were still capable of carrying out their role. Here, Admiral Cunningham's flagship *Warspite* (left), a Queen Elizabeth-class battleship, is seen berthed in Malta next to two D/E-class destroyers.

ROYAL NAVY

Although the battleships of the Mediterranean Fleet were of World War I vintage, they had all been modernized before the outbreak of the war, although work on *Valiant* was only completed in November 1939. *Warspite* and *Valiant* were more extensively improved than *Barham*, which was last modernized in the early 1930s. They all, though, possessed a powerful main armament of eight 15-inch/42 Mark I guns apiece, in four twin turrets, as well as secondary and AA batteries. They had also been converted to carry aircraft, and *Warspite*'s Fairey Swordfish floatplane poved particularly valuable during the battle. Their main batteries were well served by a modern fire-control system, and with the High Angle Control System (HACS) anti-aircraft fire-control system.

The 15-inch/42 Mark I guns mounted in these battleships were formidable weapons, even though they were first designed in 1912. They fired a 1,938lb (879kg) armour-piercing shell, with a muzzle velocity of 2,467 feet per second (752mps), and at a maximum elevation of 30° they had a range of up to 29,000 yards (26,520m), the equivalent of almost 15 miles. At that range flight time was over a minute, but at the range they fired at Matapan, the flight time was around 6 seconds. This, though, was only as good as the fire-control system that supported it. British rangefinders were reliable and accurate, and the analog computer plotting systems used had been upgraded before the war, and were now as good as any in the world. At the Battle of Calabria nine months before, *Warspite* successfully hit her target, the Italian battleship *Giulio Cesare*, at a range of 26,000 yards – testimony to the accuracy of both her guns and her fire-control system.

The British battle fleet under way. These are all Queen Elizabeth-class battleships, of World War I vintage, but modernized between the wars. *Valiant* is in the foreground, followed by *Queen Elizabeth* and then *Barham*.

Just as notably, though, *Valiant* was also fitted with a Type 279 surface-search RDF (or radar) set, which in theory had a detection range for large targets of up to 16 miles. Surface-search radar was still a rare commodity in the Mediterranean Fleet, and this made the battleship a particularly effective asset to Cunningham. She also carried the Type 284 gunnery radar, which in theory permitted radar-guided fire for her main batteries, although this system still had not been perfected. She also carried a Type 79B air-search radar, which was of limited effectiveness, but could at least detect clusters of high-flying aircraft at a range of over 80 miles. The other two battleships still hadn't acquired radar, but good communication links with *Valiant* partially overcame this. The carrier *Formidable* also carried a Type 279 set. In Pridham-Wippell's cruiser force, only *Ajax* was fitted with a Type 279 radar. This detected the Italian cruiser *Pola* in the dark at a range of 6 miles.

The British light cruisers at Matapan were all of a reasonably modern design, all entering service during the 1930s. They were armed with 6-inch/50

The Leander-class cruiser *Ajax* formed part of Pridham-Wippell's Force B during the Matapan operation. She was the only cruiser in the force to carry radar, and during the evening her Type 279 set was used to locate the crippled *Pola* in the dark.

The Fairey Swordfish was well thought of by the Fleet Air Arm, and despite its obsolete appearance, it remained in service until the end of the war. At Matapan it formed part of the air strikes launched from *Formidable* and Maleme, and was also used in a reconnaissance role.

The Fairey Albacore was the successor to the Swordfish, and like its predecessor it could function as a reconnaissance aircraft as well as a torpedo-bomber. At Matapan the Albacores embarked in *Formidable* formed the greater part of the aircraft used in the carrier's three air strikes.

Mark XXIII guns in four twin turrets, or in the case of *Gloucester* four triple turrets. These guns entered service in 1930, and fired a 112lb (50.8kg) shell, which had a maximum range of 25,450 yards (23,300m), or 12½ miles. Like any naval gun, though, the chances of hitting improved as the range dropped, and at Matapan *Gloucester* was hard-pressed to hit the enemy at 23,500 yards, which was regarded as the limit of her effective range. The advantage of these guns, though, was that while the guns were loaded mechanically, the system could be overriden, and the shells could be loaded by hand. The 6-inch shell was capable of being manually loaded at a slightly faster rate in this manner, at least until the gun crews became too fatigued to continue.

The real hitting power of the British fleet at Matapan, though, lay in the torpedo-bombers embarked in *Formidable*. Both the Fairey Swordfish and its successor the Fairey Albacore were biplanes, and looked like aircraft from an earlier era. This reflected the low priority given to Fleet Air Arm aircraft design during the interwar years. The only real advantage of the Albacore, at least for her crew, was that it had an enclosed cockpit. Both of these types of aircraft could be used as torpedo-bombers or also as reconnaissance planes. This made them versatile, which was doubly important given the relatively small number embarked in *Formidable*. They both had a cruising speed of 90–100 knots, but this was reduced when carrying a torpedo, and a ceiling of 12,000–15,000 feet. They both had an endurance of around 5 hours, although this could be extended by leaving the third crewman – the telegraphist/rear gunner – behind, and fitting a long-range fuel tank in his seat.

These torpedo-bombers each carried a single 18-inch (45cm) Mark XII aerial torpedo, which carried an explosive charge of 388lb (176kg). It could be set to a variety of depths, and had a range of up to 3,500 yards (3,200m) at 37 knots. The trouble was, these biplanes had to drop their torpedo from a height of less than 100 feet, while pointing directly at their aiming point – usually well ahead of the ship they were targeting. This meant flying straight and level, into the face of enemy AA fire. Also embarked was the Fairey Fulmar, a two-seater fighter with a cruising speed of 150 knots, and a maximum speed of up to 230 knots. It had a more impressive ceiling of 26,000 feet, allowing it to intercept high-flying bombers, and an endurance of up to 6 hours. The Fulmars were armed with machine guns, which at Matapan were used to strafe the Italian ships, as a means of distracting the gunners. This, though, was almost as dangerous a tactic as attacking a battleship in a biplane.

ORDERS OF BATTLE

ITALIAN REGIA MARINA
Commander-in-Chief Admiral Iachino

MAIN FORCE

Admiral Iachino
Vittorio Veneto (fleet flagship) (Littorio-class battleship)
Accompanying destroyers – 13th Destroyer Flotilla:
    Alpino, Bersagliere, Fuciliere, Granatiere (Soldati-class destroyers)

1ST CRUISER DIVISION

Vice Admiral Cattaneo
Zara (flagship), *Fiume, Pola* (Zara-class heavy cruisers)
Accompanying destroyers – 9th Destroyer Flotilla:
    Vittorio Alfieri, Giosuè Carducci, Vincenzo Gioberti, Alfredo Oriani
    (Oriani-class destroyers)

BRITISH ROYAL NAVY
Commander-in-Chief Admiral Cunningham

FORCE A

Admiral Cunningham, the battle fleet
Warspite (fleet flagship) (Queen Elizabeth-class battleship)
1st Battle Squadron (Rear Admiral Rawlings)
Barham (flagship), *Valiant* (Queen Elizabeth-class battleships)
Carrier Strike Force (Rear Admiral Boyd)
Formidable (flagship) (Illustrious-class fleet aircraft carrier)
Accompanying destroyers – 14th Destroyer Flotilla:
    Jervis (flotilla flag), *Janus* (J-class destroyers), *Mohawk, Nubian*
    (Tribal-class destroyers)

FORCE B

Vice Admiral Pridham-Wippell, light forces
Orion (flagship), *Ajax* (Leander-class light cruisers)
Gloucester (Gloucester-class light cruiser), *Perth* (Perth-class light
    cruiser, Royal Australian Navy vessel)
Accompanying destroyers – 2nd Destroyer Flotilla:
    Ilex (flotilla flagship), *Hasty, Hereward* (G/H/I-class destroyers),
    Vendetta (V-class destroyer, Royal Australian Navy vessel)

FORCE C

Captain Waller RAN
Stuart (flagship) (Scott-class destroyer, Royal Australian Navy
    vessel)
Greyhound, Griffin, Hostpur, Havock (G/H/I-class destroyers)

ALSO AVAILABLE

Force D in Piraeus: *Juno, Jaguar* (J-class destroyers), *Defender*
    (D-class destroyer)
On patrol in Aegean: *Rover* (Rainbow-class submarine), *Triumph*
    (Triton-class submarine)

8TH CRUISER DIVISION

Rear Admiral Legnani; attached to Cattaneo's command
Luigi di Savoia Duca degli Abruzzi (flagship), *Giuseppe Garibaldi*
    (Abruzzi-class light cruisers)
Accompanying destroyers – 16th Destroyer Flotilla:
    Emanuele Pessagno, Nicoloso da Recco (Navigatori-class
    destroyers)

3RD CRUISER DIVISION

Vice Admiral Sansonetti
Trieste (flagship), *Trento* (Trento-class heavy cruisers), *Bolzano*
    (Bolzano-class heavy cruiser)
Accompanying destroyers – 12th Destroyer Flotilla:
    Ascari, Carabiniere, Corazziere (Soldati-class destroyers)

Rear Admiral Bernard Rawlings commanded the 1st Battle Squadron, Britain's battle fleet in the Mediterranean, and flew his flag in the battleship *Barham*. At Matapan, though, operational control of the battle fleet was ceded to Cunningham, who accompanied it in *Warspite*.

OPPOSING PLANS

REGIA MARINA

As early as 15 March, Admiral Iachino had been called to Rome, to be briefed on a potential sortie into the Eastern Mediterranean. He was expected to sweep as far east as Crete, in an attempt to disrupt the British convoys operating between Egypt and Greece. Air cover for the operation would be provided by the X Corpo Aereo Tedesco – the Italian name for the German X.Fliegerkorps. They would fly from the German airfields in Sicily, and would range east across the Ionian Sea for up to 350 miles. This would equate to the longitude line of 21° East, some 120 miles from the western coast of Crete. Beyond that, air cover was promised by the Regio Aeronautica, operating from airfields near Taranto, and on Rhodes and the Dodecanese. These would cover the area as far as Crete itself, and provide long-range reconnaissance.

The Italian Zara-class heavy cruiser *Fiume* formed part of Vice Admiral Cattaneo's cruiser division at Matapan – a formation the British designated 'Force Z'. This sleek, well-designed warship, though, was destroyed within minutes during the night action stage of the Battle of Matapan.

Four days later, German Naval Intelligence informed the Supermarina that at that time, the British Mediterranean fleet contained only one fully operational battleship, *Valiant*. It added that the situation for the Italian fleet was favourable, particularly given the intense traffic between Greece and Egypt. It added: 'German Naval Command considers that the appearance of Italian units in the area south of Crete will seriously interfere with British shipping, and may even lead to the complete interruption of the transport of troops, especially as these transports are at the moment inadequately protected.' While this might have been completely incorrect in terms of the strength of the British battle fleet, it was a fair summation of the potential vulnerability of the *Lustre* convoys.

Then, on 24 May, while aboard the *Vittorio Veneto* in Naples, Admiral Iachino received his orders from the Supermarina. They directed him to put to sea, to 'attack enemy traffic on the Greece to Alexandria route, passing

This photograph was taken from the light cruiser *Garibaldi* in the forenoon of 27 March, as Cattaneo's cruisers steamed westward through the Ionian Sea. The leading ship is Cattaneo's flagship *Zara*, followed in order by *Pola*, *Fiume* and the *Abruzzi*.

westwards of Crete.' They continued: 'All merchant ships that may be sighted in the area to the west and south of Crete, or in the Aegean, must be sunk on sight.' It then added a section that would limit Iachino's ability to carry out these orders effectively. It read: 'In case of sighting enemy warships, they are to be closely engaged only if the relative conditions of strength are available.' Arguably, it meant that not only should Iachino withdraw in the face of superior enemy forces, but he should also risk engaging the enemy even when there was an approximate parity of strength. This risk-averse attitude of the Supermarina originated at the top. Mussolini was proud of his navy, and was extremely reluctant to risk it unnecessarily.

Iachino and his staff drew up their operational plan, and then, on the afternoon of 25 May, he promulgated his written orders to the relevant senior officers under his command. These included Vice Admiral Sansonetti on board *Trieste* in Messina, Sicily, who commanded the 3rd Cruiser Division; the commander of the 1st Cruiser Division Vice Admiral Cattaneo aboard *Zara* in Taranto, Apulia; and Vice Admiral Legnani aboard the light cruiser *Abruzzi*, in Brindisi, Apulia, who commanded the 8th Cruiser Division. Orders were also sent to the commanders of various destroyer flotillas: the 6th in Brindisi, the 9th in Taranto, the 10th in Naples and the 12th in Messina. So, before midnight on 25 May, all of these forces were aware of the mission ahead of them. The following day these commanders briefed their ship commanders. In all, Iachino planned to put to sea with a force of 22 warships: one battleship, six heavy cruisers, two light cruisers and 13 destroyers.

When Iachino's flagship sailed from Naples on the evening of 26 March, this sortie began in earnest. In three other Italian ports naval forces were also busily loading stores and ammunition, or preparing for sea. Their departures were timed to coincide with the *Vittorio Veneto*'s passage eastwards. There were, though, some elements added by Iachino and his staff to the original plan. Once the fleet reached the waters to the south-west of Crete, Cattaneo, Legnani and the 8th and 9th Destroyer flotillas would be sent north, to pass through the Antikithera Channel before dawn on 28 March. Under Cattaneo's command they would then sweep the southern Aegean, venturing as far as the north-eastern tip of Crete. If no contact was made, they would then return the way they had come, and pass back through the channel at around noon.

The previous evening, though, an hour before Cattaneo was due to sail, this additional element to the sweep was cancelled on the orders of the Supermarina. Instead, Cattaneo would join the main sweep to the south of Crete. Iachino later attributed this amendment to his plan to the sighting of Sansonetti's cruisers by an RAF Sunderland a little after noon that day. The Supermarina, Iachino felt, was now convinced that the enemy convoys would be rerouted, and so it was placing Cattaneo's force in danger by venturing that far to the east. Still, by the evening of 27 March all of Iachino's forces were at sea, and by dawn they would be perfectly placed to carry out their sweep, a little to the south of Crete's south-western tip.

ROYAL NAVY

The fleet aircraft carrier *Formidable* was the most important asset available to Admiral Cunningham during the Matapan operation. Although it had a pitifully small air wing embarked, Cunningham was determined to use her aircraft to slow down the enemy sufficiently so that he could engage them with his battle fleet.

Cunningham intended to intercept Admiral Iachino's fleet somewhere to the west of Crete some time after dawn on 28 March. His 'eyes and ears' would be his deputy, Vice Admiral Pridham-Wippell. Although he only had four light cruisers and four destroyers under his command, this was a reasonably strong scouting force. For the operation, it was designated as Force B. By then, Cunningham hoped to be approaching from the south-east with the aircraft carrier *Formidable* and her embarked aircraft forming part of his battle fleet. The battle fleet would consist of three battleships, the carrier and four escorting destroyers. This would be Force A. Cunningham expected to be within flying range of Force B by dawn. So, *Formidable* would launch search aircraft, which would assist Pridham-Wippell in locating the enemy fleet. A third group, designated Force C and consisting of five destroyers, had

The Australian light cruiser *Perth* formed part of Force B at Matapan. She was one of two Royal Australian Navy warships to take part in the battle. This shows her in the striking camouflage scheme she bore in the spring of 1941.

sailed from Alexandria with the battle fleet, but would be detached during the night, with orders to make contact with Pridham-Wippell at dawn.

In addition, three destroyers were in Piraeus, where they had been waiting to form the escort of the southbound *Lustre* convoy. They would now become Force D, and could be called upon if Cunningham needed them. Finally, two submarines were on patrol in the Aegean at the time, and these, too, could be brought under Cunningham's control if required. There was a small Fleet Air Arm contingent from 815 Naval Air Squadron (NAS) at Maleme airfield in Crete, consisting of five Swordfish torpedo-bombers/reconnaissance planes, formerly embarked in *Illustrious*. Cunningham had also notified RAF Greece Command, based north of Athens, which would assist him by operating reconnaissance flights over the Ionian Sea and the waters around Crete, while also maintaining Blenheim bombers in readiness to launch bombing attacks on naval targets if requested. Finally, the small Greek navy would be notified if the Italians tried to enter the Aegean, and would sail to intercept them.

On the afternoon of 26 March, Cunningham issued his general orders for the operation to his senior commanders. They stated:

1.   Force B consisting of four cruisers and destroyers (*Orion*, *Ajax*, *Perth*, *Gloucester*, *Ilex*, *Hasty*, *Hereward* and *Vendetta*) under Vice Admiral, Light Forces, to be south-west of Gavdos Island off Crete at daylight on 28 March.

2.   Force C consisting of five destroyers (*Stuart*, *Greyhound*, *Griffin*, *Hotspur* and *Havock*) to join Force B at daylight on 28 March.

It was really that simple. As Cunningham himself put it later: 'It was designed to give flexibility and allowed for a quick change of plan if more intelligence came to hand. Essentially, though, this flexibility was the key to Cunningham's plans. His intent was, if possible, to catch Iachino, and to deal a crippling blow to his surface fleet. He could only do that if both he and his subordinates were ready to act on their initiative, and to do so with both decisiveness and daring.

The opening moves, 0600–0900hrs, 28 March

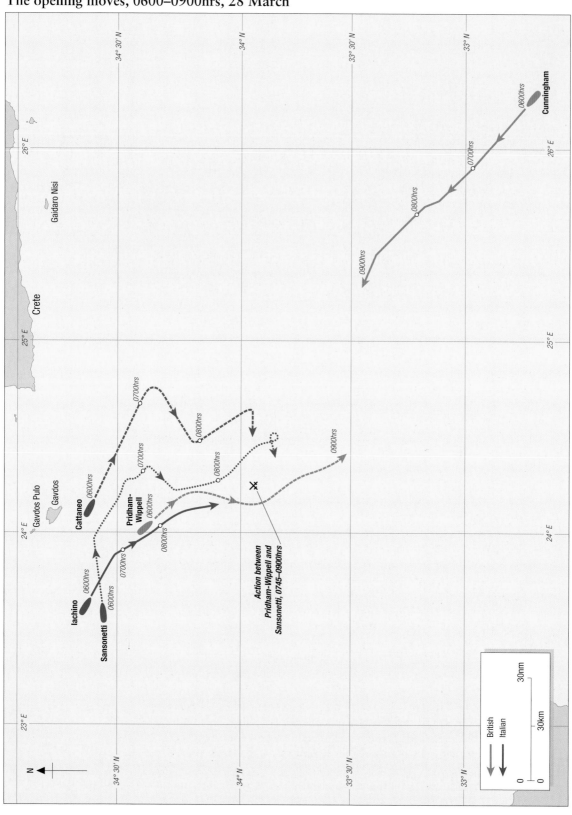

THE BATTLE OF CAPE MATAPAN

FIRST CONTACT

Sunrise that morning was at 0720hrs, but the pre-dawn nautical twilight began almost an hour earlier, at 0625hrs. While it was still dark, an Ro.43 floatplane was launched from the *Vittorio Veneto*, watched by Admiral Iachino. Without radar, aircraft like this served as the eyes and ears of the Italian battle fleet. At the time, the battleship was 15 miles to the west of the small Greek island of Gavdos, and 25 miles south of the south-western corner of Crete. With her screen of four destroyers around her, she was on a south-easterly heading, making 20 knots. The biplane climbed, and as the light began to improve to the east, it ranged ahead of the battleship, her pilot and observer trying to spot the telltale white phosphorescent wake of enemy warships. Then, at 0635hrs, they saw them, several miles to the south-south-west. They closed to investigate, and soon were radioing a sighting report to their battleship. It noted that a British force of four cruisers and two destroyers had been spotted to the south of Gavdos, and was heading towards the south-east.

Iachino now knew that at least part of the British fleet was at sea. His latest intelligence reports still placed Admiral Cunningham and his battleships in Alexandria, so the chances were these cruisers were there to escort a convoy to Greece, or were simply conducting a sweep in the Ionian Sea. In either case he planned to bring them to battle. In that pre-dawn twilight, though, *Vittorio Veneto*'s floatplane wasn't the only aircraft out looking for the enemy. At 0445hrs four Swordfish had taken off from Maleme airfield in Crete, and flown west, fanning out across the Ionian Sea. One of them had to turn back with engine trouble, but the others continued their sweep. They found nothing, and were all back at Maleme by 0845hrs. On board the light cruiser *Orion*, the Italian floatplane had been spotted. This told Pridham-Wippell that at least one Italian cruiser or even a battleship was somewhere in the area.

Earlier, Pridham-Wippell had detached the destroyers *Ilex* and *Hasty* to extend his pre-dawn search area closer to Gavdos. So, when they rejoined him at 0645hrs, the eight British warships turned south onto a new course of 200°. That took them away from the most probable location of the Italian ship that had launched the floatplane. Meanwhile, Cunningham's battle fleet was roughly 170 miles to the south-east of Pridham-Wippell, on a north-westerly course of 310°, making 16 knots. At 0555hrs, *Formidable* launched

The Leander-class light cruiser *Orion* served as the flagship of Vice Admiral Pridham-Wippell, who commanded the Mediterranean Fleet's light forces. While her 6-inch guns were no match for Sansonetti's heavier cruisers, he was determined to maintain close contact with his opponent.

five search aircraft, plus an anti-submarine patrol aircraft and two combat air patrol Fulmar fighters. The searching Swordfish spread out in a fan-shaped search pattern which extended as far as 23° East, and ranging as far north as the west coast of Crete. At 0720hrs, just as the sun rose over the eastern horizon, aircraft 5B sighted the enemy. Two minutes later the plane radioed in her sighting report – four enemy cruisers and four destroyers, 42 miles to the south-east of Gavdos. The Italian ships were heading towards the south-west, away from the coast of Crete.

Another report came in at 0729hrs. This time, aircraft 5F spotted four cruisers and six destroyers, 20 miles ahead of the other ships. In fact, the observer of 5F mistook his position, and was about 15 miles north of where he thought he was. *Formidable* quickly passed the news on to Cunningham. On board *Warspite* the British admiral was delighted that what seemed to be two enemy cruiser forces had been sighted, both to the south-east of Gavdos. It was just as well Pridham-Wippell had changed course, or he could have been caught between them. Still, Cunningham knew that the air crews weren't infallible. Navigational errors could creep in, and although visibility was reportedly 15 miles, patches of mist could hinder accurate identification. Were these both Italian forces? Were they one single enemy force? Or had the searchers merely sighted Pridham-Wippell's ships? In fact, the Swordfish had sighted two separate Italian forces, some 25 miles apart – Force Z to the south-east of Gavdos, and Force X, 25 miles due west of it and south-south-east of Gavdos. That placed Force X on course to intercept Pridham-Wippell.

Sure enough, at 0745hrs lookouts on Pridham-Wippell's flagship *Orion* sighted smoke almost directly astern of them, on a bearing of 010°. A minute later their hulls became visible 16 miles away, and they were identified as Italian heavy cruisers. Pridham-Wippell increased speed to 28 knots, but the enemy cruisers were seen to draw closer. That meant they were faster than he was. So, at 0752hrs he altered course again, this time to the south-east. That way he could draw the enemy cruisers onto the guns of the British battle fleet, some 90 miles away, but closing fast. The British cruiser commander would have been less sanguine if he had known that not only was a second Italian cruiser force just over the horizon to the north-east, but the *Vittorio Veneto* was astern of him, not far from Gavdos, and could intercept the British cruisers if they turned away towards the west. It was a tough spot to be in, especially as the guns of the Italian cruisers had the edge in range.

The Italians spotted the British cruisers at the same time, and Vice Admiral Sansonetti in *Trieste* ordered his ships to turn to port, onto a course that was

A detail of the Italian heavy cruiser *Trieste*, flagship of Vice Admiral Sansonetti during the Battle of Cape Matapan. This view shows her forward main battery, but also her bridge, compass platform and fire control directors on her foremast, and above her bridge.

almost parallel to the British, but converged slightly. That was to ensure that all his guns could bear on the enemy. Also, with the slightly converging course and their greater speed, the range dropped steadily. The 20.3cm (8-inch) guns of the Italian heavy cruisers had a maximum range of 28,000m (30,620 yards) at 45° of elevation. *Bolzano*, with her slightly improved Model 1927 guns, had an even longer maximum range of 31,566m (34,521 yards). That meant Sansonetti had to close to within 14 miles to have a chance of hitting the enemy. For their part, the 6-inch cruisers of Pridham-Wippell's command had a maximum range of just 25,480 yards, or 23,300m. Consequently, the range had to drop to 12 miles before the British could fire back.

Meanwhile, at 0804hrs, another radio report from Swordfish 5B reached *Formidable*, confirming the other enemy force consisted of four cruisers and six destroyers. Their location was well to the north-east of Pridham-Wippell's reported position, and over the horizon from him. As he was already in contact with an enemy force of three heavy cruisers, escorted by three destroyers, there were clearly two groups of Italian cruisers at sea south of Crete. This mollified Cunningham, who now had a better idea of what he and his light cruiser commander were facing. Meanwhile, Sansonetti's cruisers were drawing steadily closer to the British. Then, at 0812hrs, when the range had dropped to 22,000m, he turned his ships onto a parallel course to Pridham-Wippell, and gave the order to open fire. These were the opening shots of the battle.

At that range, the chances of scoring a hit were slim. Later, Admiral Iachino offered an explanation for the lack of effectiveness of his cruisers' salvoes:

> The *Trieste* Division opened fire at 22,000m, and the first salvoes fell very short … the distance between the two groups was in fact never less than 24,000m. Atmospheric conditions were most unfavourable for rangefinding at great distance, especially with the old rangefinders fitted in the *Trento* and *Trieste*. These instruments actually did not succeed in giving any reading before opening fire, and afterwards their readings were jumpy, uncertain and inaccurate.

On the British side the four light cruisers all aimed their own guns at the enemy, and Pridham-Wippell allowed ship captains to return fire if they deemed it worthwhile.

FIRST ENCOUNTER, 0830HRS, 28 MARCH 1941 (PP. 32–33)

Soon after dawn on 28 March a British search aircraft sighted a group of three Italian heavy cruisers off the south-western corner of Crete. Vice Admiral Pridham-Wippell was nearby, with a squadron of four British light cruisers, but it was shortly before 0800hrs when his lookouts spotted the enemy. He immediately turned away, hoping to lead the Italian cruisers onto the guns of the main British fleet. Vice Admiral Sansonetti in *Trieste* ordered his ships to give chase, and soon the two groups of warships were running southwards, away from the Cretan coast.

At 0812hrs *Trieste* (**1**) opened fire, followed soon after by the heavy cruisers *Trento* and *Bolzano*. The three accompanying Italian destroyers (**2**) didn't join in, as their guns lacked the range. At that point the two groups of cruisers were 12 miles apart. The

Italian 8-inch shells began falling short of the British ships, and no hits were scored. Gradually, though, their gunnery improved until the shells were falling around the rearmost British ships (**3**).

Then, at 0829hrs, the last of the British ships, the light cruiser *Gloucester*, opened fire at the enemy with her twelve 6-inch guns (**4**). The range, though, was 23,500 yards – just beyond maximum effective range – and her three salvoes fell short. This prompted Sansonetti to order an alteration of course to starboard, to stay out of range of the lighter British guns. Rather than waste shells, Pridham-Wippell ordered *Gloucester* to cease fire. The Italian ships, though, continued firing until 0855hrs, when they finally ceased fire and turned away. While this exchange of fire might have been ineffective, these salvoes were the opening shots of the battle.

Although the Italian shells all fell far short of them, it soon became clear that the Italians were targeting the rearmost British ship – the light cruiser *Gloucester*. Her commanding officer, Captain Rowley, ordered his ship to zig-zag, to throw off the enemy gunners. By 0829hrs Rowley noted that the range had now dropped to 23,500 yards (21,488m), or just over 11½ miles. That meant the enemy were now within range. So, *Gloucester* fired three salvoes in quick succession, targeting the *Trento*, at the head of the Italian line. She even launched her aircraft, partly to reduce the risk of fire, but also to help improve the accuracy of her own gunnery. The 6-inch salvoes all fell short, but they were close enough to encourage the Italians to react. Despite their firepower, these Italian cruisers were poorly protected, and so Sansonetti felt it prudent to turn away to widen the range. Once beyond 24,000m he turned his line back onto its parallel course, and resumed firing, while staying safely out of range of the lighter British guns.

Pridham-Wippell held his nerve, though, and continued running at high speed towards the south-east. Each minute brought him closer to Cunningham's battle fleet, and he hoped he could draw Sansonetti within range of its powerful guns. Then, at 0854hrs, the situation changed abruptly. *Formidable* had forwarded a sighting report to *Orion* which made uncomfortable reading for the British cruiser commander. It was from Swordfish 5F, which reported sighting three Italian battleships to the south of Gavdos. The report had been sent at 0805hrs, and Pridham-Wippell knew it to be 'manifestly incorrect', as at the time of the sighting *Orion* had been only 7 miles from the reported position of the battleships. While this was an error in navigation, the report that three Italian battleships might be nearby was disquieting. More likely, though, they were three large cruisers – undoubtedly Sansonetti's command.

At 0830hrs Pridham-Wippell had turned his line slightly to starboard, so he was now running more to the south-south-east. Seven minutes later Sansonetti turned onto a parallel course, still keeping out of range of the British guns. This one-sided but ineffectual engagement continued until 0855hrs, when Sansonetti ordered his ships to cease fire. He had become concerned that the British were leading him farther away from the two other Italian naval groups, and was rightly alert to the fact that he might be heading into a trap. So, he ordered his ships to break off, turning in a circle to port, before steaming off towards the north-west at 28 knots, on a course of 300°. Effectively, they were now heading directly towards the protection offered by the *Vittorio Veneto*.

In British warships, gunnery was controlled from the Gunnery Control Tower. This wartime diagram shows the way this was manned and operated, with rangefinding and spotting staff ready to pass on the information to the guns by way of the ship's plotting room.

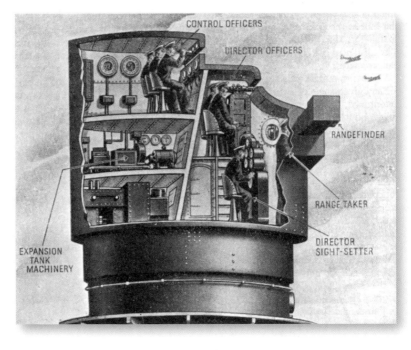

CONTROL OFFICERS

DIRECTOR OFFICERS

RANGEFINDER

RANGE TAKER

DIRECTOR SIGHT-SETTER

EXPANSION TANK MACHINERY

ITALIAN

A. 3rd Cruiser Division (Vice Admiral Sansonetti)
  – designated Force X by British:
  heavy cruisers *Trieste* (flag), *Trento* and *Bolzano*
Accompanied by 12th Destroyer Flotilla:
  destroyers *Ascari*, *Carabiniere* and *Corazziere*

B. 1st Cruiser Division (Vice Admiral Cattaneo) –
  designated Force Z by British:
  heavy cruisers *Zara* (flag), *Fiume* and *Pola*
Accompanied by 9th Destroyer Flotilla:
  destroyers *Alfieri*, *Carducci*, *Gioberti* and *Oriani*
With 8th Cruiser Division (Rear Admiral Legnani):
  light cruisers *Duca degli Abruzzi* (flag) and
  Giuseppe Garibaldi
Accompanied by 16th Destroyer Flotilla:
  destroyers *Emanuele Pessagno* and *Nicoloso
  da Recco*

B 0720HRS

0730

3
SANSONETTI

1
CATTANEO

A 0720HRS

0730HRS

0745HRS

080

GAVDOS

EVENTS

1. Lookouts in *Orion* sight Sansonetti's force to the north, and Force B steers away.

2. After using their superior speed to overhaul the British, Sansonetti's cruisers open fire at the British at 0812hrs, firing at extreme range (22,000m). No hits are scored.

3. At 0829hrs the rearmost ship in the British line, *Gloucester*, returns fire with three salvoes, targeting *Trieste*. Again, no hits are achieved.

4. At 0830hrs, as Pridham-Wippell turns his force to the south-south-east, to lure Sansonetti towards the British battle fleet 75nm to the south-east, *Gloucester* launches her floatplane to shadow the Italian force.

5. At 0837hrs, Sansonetti takes the bait and turns onto a parallel course to the British.

6. Cattaneo's combined force comes within visual range of Sansonetti. He alters course to the west, to screen the Italian flagship, which is then 25nm to the west of Gavdos, leaving Sansonetti to continue the pursuit of Pridham-Wippell. At 0917hrs, *Gloucester*'s floatplane sights Cattaneo's force, but the sighting report is never forwarded to either Pridham-Wippell or Admiral Cunningham, who is leading the main battle fleet on a course to intercept Sansonetti.

7. At 0855hrs, Sansonetti orders his cruisers to cease fire. He then turns his force to port, before settling on a westerly course, to maintain contact with both Cattaneo and Admiral Iachino in the fleet flagship.

8. By 0900hrs, the British battle fleet is 75nm from Force B. When he sees Sansonetti break contact and turn away to the west, Pridham-Wippell turns towards the north, before pursuing Sansonetti. At this stage he remains unaware that Cattaneo's force is in the area.

0   10   20

NAUTICAL MILE

THE ACTION OFF GAVDOS, 0630–0900HRS, 28 MARCH

The action off Gavdos Island, lying to the south of Crete's south-western tip, was little more than a skirmish, fought at long range. It did, though, mark the opening shots of the Battle of Matapan. After Pridham-Wippell and Sansonetti's forces sighted each other, the British ran southwards, in an attempt to lure the Italians onto the guns of Admiral Cunningham's battle fleet, which was approaching from the south-east. Using his ships' superior speed, Sansonetti closed the range, and engaged them at long distance. Although no hits were scored, when *Gloucester* fired back, the Italian commander decided to keep his distance, rather than close the range further, and so put his ships at risk. Eventually, rather than be drawn farther away from the rest of the fleet, Sansonetti broke contact, and so avoided falling into the British trap.

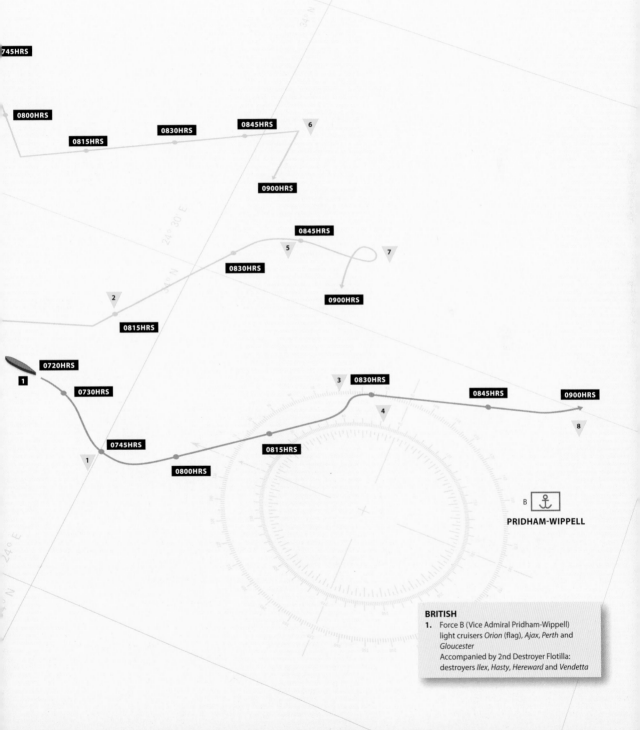

B ⚓

PRIDHAM-WIPPELL

BRITISH
1. Force B (Vice Admiral Pridham-Wippell)
    light cruisers *Orion* (flag), *Ajax*, *Perth* and
    Gloucester
    Accompanied by 2nd Destroyer Flotilla:
    destroyers *Ilex*, *Hasty*, *Hereward* and *Vendetta*

By 0900hrs that morning the first phase of the battle was over. Pridham-Wippell had performed well, but he now knew that at least one other enemy force was somewhere to the north of him, while a possible force of Italian battleships was somewhere between him and Gavdos. The danger now was that he would be led into a trap of Iachino's making. Like Sansonetti, Pridham-Wippell had his own supporting battleships. By 0900hrs Cunningham's battle fleet was 72 miles away to the south-east, making 20 knots. So, Pridham-Wippell turned north again, hoping to resume his role as the scouting force for the battle fleet. This proved more successful than he'd hoped. *Gloucester*'s Walrus floatplane was still in the air to the north of the British cruisers. At 0917hrs she radioed in her own sighting report, as her crew had spotted another force of Italian cruisers, approaching from the north-east. This was clearly the enemy force sighted by *Formidable*'s Swordfish an hour before.

This was Force Z, commanded by Vice Admiral Cattaneo. His flagship *Zara* and her sister ship *Fiume* had the same advantage in range over the British that Sansonetti's cruisers had enjoyed. They were also accompanied by the light cruisers *Abruzzi* and *Garibaldi*, and six destroyers. However, due to transmission problems, the sighting report from the Walrus never reached Pridham-Wippell. At 0921hrs he had turned his force to port, and was now racing off after Sansonetti's cruisers. The hope was that he could maintain contact with them, and so guide Cunningham towards the enemy. Before he altered course, though, Pridham-Wippell detached one of his destroyers, the *Vendetta*, which had developed engine trouble. She set off towards Alexandria on her own, while her companions steamed away to the west, chasing Sansonetti. Despite not receiving *Gloucester*'s sighting report, Pridham-Wippell knew a second group of enemy cruisers was somewhere close by, probably to the north or north-east of him. That meant that if he turned back now, it was possible that these could cut him off from the British battle fleet. Still, he had no firm idea where they were, while he knew where Sansonetti was, and in which direction he was going. So, he kept following him. At 0936hrs Pridham-Wippell was finally rewarded by a sighting of the enemy cruisers 15 miles ahead of him. He turned his force onto the same north-westerly heading as the Italians, and doggedly followed them.

PURSUITS AND AMBUSHES

The three groups of Italian ships were scattered across the Ionian Sea, to the south of Gavdos. Sansonetti's Force X was heading towards the north-west at 28 knots, and by 0930hrs was roughly in the same patch of sea as Pridham-Wippell had been when the Italians had first opened fire on *Gloucester*. At that moment Cattaneo's Force Z was just in sight some 14 miles away to the north-east. After being spotted by *Gloucester*'s Walrus, Cattaneo had also turned his ships towards the north-west, and so he, too, was heading towards the third Italian group. This comprised Admiral Iachino in *Vittorio Veneto*, and her small escort of destroyers. The battleship and her screen of four destroyers were 18 miles south-east of Gavdos, steering towards the south-south-east. That put Iachino roughly 15 miles west of Cattaneo, and 25 miles north-west of Sansonetti. If they were threatened, the Italians could combine their forces, or else use the cruisers to screen the precious battleship.

The battleship *Barham*, sister ship of *Warspite* and *Valiant*, was the least extensively modernized of the three Queen Elizabeth-class battleships. During the Matapan operation her engines could only make a maximum of 22 knots, almost 3 knots less than her sisters.

Meanwhile, Pridham-Wippell was 15 miles astern of Sansonetti, and about 18 miles south of Cattaneo, whose force was just out of sight of the British cruisers. Cunningham's battle fleet was 72 miles to the south-east, approaching at 24 knots. Earlier, *Warspite* had suffered from engine problems which had reduced her speed. So, at 0851hrs he detached *Valiant* and sent her on ahead at 24 knots, accompanied by the destroyers *Nubian* and *Mohawk*. His aim was to support Pridham-Wippell. By 0900hrs, though, the problem with the flagship's condenser had been fixed, and *Valiant* and her escorts rejoined the flagship. Even then, *Barham*, the slowest of the three battleships, could only make 22 knots, so at 0918hrs a frustrated Cunningham reluctantly reduced speed to ensure his battle fleet remained together.

Meanwhile, on the carrier Rear Admiral Denis Boyd had been ordered to prepare to launch an air strike. Cunningham's order was given at 0833hrs, but it took time to range the torpedo-carrying aircraft on deck, and to arm them. A Fairey Albacore had an effective speed of around 90 knots when carrying a torpedo, and at the time the order was given the only enemy force sighted was Sansonetti's cruisers. It would take almost an hour to close with them, given their recorded position at 0900hrs. Even then there was no guarantee the strike could locate the enemy before the aircraft ran short of fuel, and had to return to their carrier. Interestingly, when a second strike was launched, the aircraft's gunner would be left behind, to make room for an extra fuel tank to extend the aircraft's endurance.

The first of *Formidable*'s air strikes of the day would consist of six Albacores, each armed with a single Mark XII torpedo. It was to be led by Lieutenant-Commander Wilfrid Saunt, the commander of 826 NAS. The torpedo-armed biplanes would be accompanied by

Rear Admiral Denis Boyd, commanding the Mediterranean Fleet's carrier strike force, flew his flag in *Formidable* – the fleet's only operational carrier. Having supervised the Taranto raid the previous November, Boyd was keen to 'finish the job' by attacking Italy's remaining operational battleship.

two Fairey Fulmars from 802 NAS, to provide them with fighter cover. Then, at 0922hrs, Cunningham ordered Boyd to delay launching the strike. At the time, the Italians had broken off their fight with Pridham-Wippell's cruisers, and Sansonetti was now withdrawing towards the north-west. That sighting report of Italian battleships gave Cunningham pause. He was well aware that his greatest advantage that morning was *Formidable* and her strike aircraft. So, he was concerned about showing his hand too early that morning, as there seemed to be at least three groups of enemy ships operating off Gavdos. However, in what was one of the most important decisions of his career, at 0939hrs Cunningham told Boyd to go ahead with the strike.

Seventeen minutes later *Formidable* turned to starboard into the wind, which was blowing from the north-east at 22 knots. By 1000hrs all eight aircraft were in the air and forming up, before heading off in search of a possible enemy battle fleet, about 80 miles ahead. At the same time, Captain Arthur Bisset of *Formidable* ordered the launch of a Swordfish from 826 NAS, to observe any surface action that might take place, and two patrolling Fulmars and two Swordfish search aircraft landed back on. This done, *Formidable* rejoined the battle fleet, which was still steaming towards the north-east in line ahead, with the flagship in the lead. Boyd estimated that it would take Saunt and his planes about an hour to reach Pridham-Wippell, and longer to locate any nearby enemy force, unless the British cruisers came upon them first.

Cunningham needed to locate the enemy. By 1000hrs Pridham-Wippell was following on the heels of Sansonetti's cruisers; both groups of ships were faster than the British battle fleet, and so both were drawing away from it. Somewhere to the north of the British cruisers was another Italian cruiser force, but contact with it had now been lost. Then there was the report of Italian battleships, also somewhere to the north of Pridham-Wippell. That, of course, depended on the questionable accuracy of a sighting report sent two hours before. If they existed, these Italian battleships could even be poised to fall upon the isolated British cruisers. So, to help him gain a better picture, Cunningham had requested that the RAF send out search aircraft from Maleme in Crete.

The Fleet Air Arm's own 815 NAS at Maleme had already failed to sight the enemy. Earlier that morning Cunningham had ordered the squadron to launch its own strike against Sansonetti's Force X. it took time for the signal to be relayed to Maleme, but eventually at 1050hrs three Swordfish took off from the airfield, armed with Mark XII torpedoes. These, though, would take around an hour to intercept Sansonetti. In the meantime, Pridham-Wippell was sending in regular reports from astern of Force X,

This wartime diagram, showing an Illustrious-class fleet carrier like *Formidable*, explains why carriers steamed into the wind for flying operations. It shows how, by taxiing into the wind, the aircraft could become airborne at a slower take-off speed. This is why, during 28 March, *Formidable* had to turn away from the battle fleet when launching or recovering aircraft.

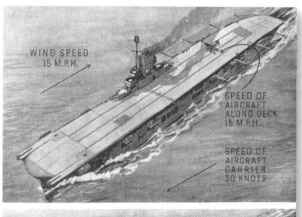

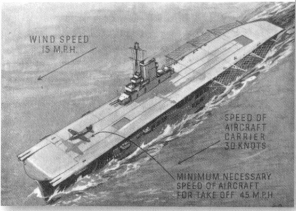

so at least both groups of British torpedo planes had a potential target. The danger lay in telling friend from foe. So, at around 1045hrs, when *Formidable*'s strike team came within sight of Pridham-Wippell's force, the British cruisers opened fire on their own aircraft. As Lieutenant Frank Hopkins, a future admiral, put it: 'In spite of our repeated attempts to identify ourselves to them, they kept up a steady barrage of AA fire at us, until we eventually passed out of range ahead of them.' Fortunately, none of *Formidable*'s aircraft were hit.

It was now almost 1100hrs. At 1058hrs, a lookout on *Orion* spotted smoke on the horizon, 16

This hastily snapped photograph taken from the Australian light cruiser shows a near miss from a 15-inch shell fired by the *Vittorio Veneto* during the attack on Force B by the battleship. In the background is the light cruiser *Gloucester*.

miles due north of them. Surprisingly, *Formidable*'s aircraft hadn't spotted this new threat. On the bridge of Pridham-Wippell's flagship, Commander Ralph Fisher of the vice admiral's staff remembered the moment a minute or so later when the approaching ship was identified. They were eating bully beef sandwiches at the time, and suddenly the ship's first lieutenant, Commander Trethowan Wynn, 'with his mouth full of sandwich, nudged me and said "What battleship is that over there on the starboard beam? I thought ours were miles to the east of us." ... As I took my binoculars to examine a vessel hull down to the northwards, there was a whistling noise, and the first salvo of 15-inch [shells] from the *Vittorio Veneto* landed somewhere around.' At the time, though, the approaching ship was officially identified as an Italian battleship of the Vittorio Veneto class.

On *Orion*'s bridge, Pridham-Wippell immediately ordered an immediate turn away from the threat by all ships. Without ado, Captain Geoffrey Back of *Orion* turned hard aport, increased speed and ordered smoke to be laid to cover his cruiser's turn to the south. Fisher, a destroyer man, later said of his wartime experience aboard light cruisers that, 'we seem to be always having to run away'. This was certainly one of those occasions. On board *Warspite*, Pridham-Wippell's radio orders to his force were intercepted, and the news passed to Cunningham even before the official sighting report reached him. He had confidence that once Pridham-Wippell had widened the range, he would attempt to shadow the enemy battleship. That would help Cunningham to attack her, either by using air strikes from *Formidable*, or, if the Italian battleship could be slowed down, by bringing his own battleships into action against her.

Admiral Iachino's ambush of Pridham-Wippell had been perfectly executed. On board *the Vittorio Veneto* signals from the British cruisers had been intercepted, and a little after 1000hrs Iachino had turned his force around to the north-west, onto a course that was roughly parallel to Sansonetti and Pridham-Wippell. At 1055hrs he made contact with Force X, and promptly hauled around to starboard, before settling on a south-

south-easterly that should bring him into contact with the shadowing British cruisers. Sure enough, lookouts on *Vittorio Veneto* spotted the enemy off their starboard beam at 1057hrs, and Iachino ordered the battleship to open fire with her forward main guns on the leading British ship – the *Orion*. The surprise was absolute. Three minutes later, on Iachino's signal, Sansonetti also turned his column of ships to port, onto a parallel course to the battleship, which was now 12 miles to the north-east of him. As the British ships turned away to the south, Sansonetti's cruisers were now well-placed to join in the attack, once they drew within range.

It was a dangerous moment for Pridham-Wippell. Sansonetti's heavy cruisers were both faster and more powerful than his own. It went without saying that the *Vittorio Veneto*, with her 38.1cm (15-inch) guns could demolish a British light cruiser with a single salvo. They also had an effective range of 35,000 yards, or just over 14 miles. Although her after turret couldn't bear, her two triple forward turrets could, and salvoes of 15-inch shells were now falling close to the British ships. The range had now dropped to 12 miles, which meant the shells had a flight time of around 40 seconds. While the Italian fire was slow but accurate, the salvoes were widely spaced, rather than closely grouped. This was later traced to a problem involving the closeness of the barrels in her triple turrets – the blast from the centre barrel forced the outer shells outwards slightly, widening the salvo spread. Still, for the British it was an unpleasant experience, especially when, at 1106hrs, *Orion* suffered a near miss which peppered her upper deck with shrapnel.

What helped the British was the commander's order to 'make smoke by all available means'. With a light wind blowing from the north-east, from the cruisers' port quarter, this black, oily funnel smoke gradually thickened into an effective screen. The only cruiser not covered by it was *Gloucester*. She had been suffering from mechanical problems, and was having trouble keeping pace with her consorts. She was also to windward of the others, and so the smokescreen was considerably less effective. At 1109hrs *Vittorio Veneto* shifted her fire from *Orion* to *Gloucester*, resulting in an improvement in accuracy. Photographs from the British ships, later published in *Life* magazine, bore testimony to that.

The light cruiser *Gloucester*, pictured while under fire from the 15-inch shells of the *Vittorio Veneto* during Pridham-Wippell's forenoon encounter with the Italian battleship. In the background is the smokescreen laid by the British cruisers.

Gloucester was straddled twice before the destroyer *Hasty* raced over to *Gloucester*'s port quarter, and weaved back and forth belching funnel smoke. This soon screened the British cruiser, and the accuracy of the Italian salvoes decreased noticeably. In all, the *Vittorio Veneto* fired 29 salvoes, mostly from one forward turret at a time. Some 11 shells failed to fire, and had to be removed from the barrels. Still, it was a deadly concentration of fire, and as the firing continued, the likelihood of scoring a crippling hit increased. Sansonetti's cruisers were gaining too, off *Orion*'s starboard quarter, and soon they would draw into range, and add the weight of their guns to the one-sided barrage. To Pridham-Wippell the situation must have seemed hopeless. Then, at 1127hrs, everything changed. What suddenly turned things around was the arrival of Lieutenant-Commander Saunt's air strike.

THE FIRST AIR STRIKES

At 1058hrs, just as the British cruisers first sighted the Italian battleship, Saunt and his observer Lieutenant Hopkins spotted the *Vittorio Veneto*. At the time, they were heading towards the south-east, flying at 9,000 feet (2,743m). Moments later they saw the battleship's salvoes begin to fall close astern of the British cruisers, which by then had turned away towards the south. Hopkins later summed up the situation:

> We sighted one large warship, escorted by four destroyers, steaming towards our cruisers, and shortly after this the large warship, which turned out to be a battleship of the Littorio class, opened fire on our cruisers ... Unless we could do something quickly, our cruisers would be picked off at long range by the *Vittorio Veneto*. The trouble was, we were all abaft the beam of the *Vittorio Veneto*. She was steaming at 30 knots, the wind at our height was 30 knots against us, so that since our air speed was only 90 knots, we were only catching up at a relative speed of 30 knots. I think it took the best part of 20 minutes to creep up to a suitable attacking position ahead of the *Vittorio Veneto*.

As this was going on, seemingly out of the blue, two German Ju 88s appeared to the east, coming out of the sun at 12,000 feet. These had flown from North Africa on a regular reconnaissance sweep, and had happened across the British air strike at a critical moment. However, as they dived to attack the torpedo-bombers, they were spotted by the two covering Fulmars. They turned and carried out a head-on attack on the two Junkers, and Lieutenant Donald Gibson's fighter shot one of them down. The other German fighter-bomber turned away. So, the attack on the battleship was able to continue unhindered, save for the formidable AA fire the Italian battleship could put up.

According to Saunt's pre-arranged plan, the attack would take place in two waves, each of three Albacores, and would attempt to attack the target simultaneously from both port and starboard. The four escorting destroyers, Saunt noted, were in line astern, half a mile off the port beam of the battleship. That meant they formed a partial screen against an attack by torpedo-bombers. As the aircraft circled round the enemy ships from the east, the five Italian warships opened up a heavy but ultimately ineffective

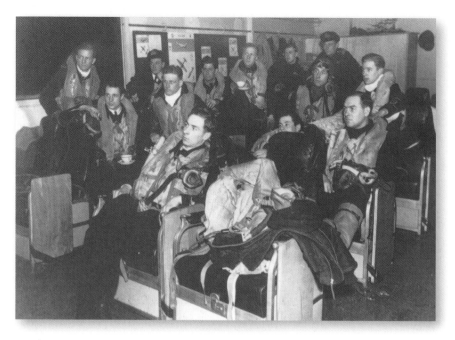

Fleet Air Arm crews attending a pre-strike briefing. These were used to outline navigational details and attack plans, reinforce ship identification and to lay out emergency procedures in the event of setbacks. Typically, they were carried out shortly before the strike was launched.

AA barrage to port. At the same time, the *Vittorio Veneto* was still firing at the British cruisers a dozen miles ahead of her.

First (Dusk) Strike – *Formidable*

Aircraft	Aircraft ID	Pilot	Observer	Telegraphist/Rear Gunner
Albacore	4A	Lieutenant-Commander Saunt	Lieutenant Hopkins	–
Albacore	4C	Sub-Lieutenant Bradshaw	Sub-Lieutenant Drummond	–
Albacore	4F	Lieutenant Ellis	Lieutenant Haworth	–
Albacore	4K	Lieutenant Abrams	Lieutenant Smith-Shand	–
Albacore	4P	Sub-Lieutenant Tuke	Sub-Lieutenant Mallett	–
Albacore	5A	Sub-Lieutenant Williams	Midshipman Davis	Leading Airman Booth

Note: All but 5A had no third crewman as they were fitted with long-range tanks instead.

Still, by 1127hrs Saunt had worked his way to a position just over a mile ahead of the battleship. He then gave the order to attack. Hopkins picked up the story: 'Eventually we got into an attacking position and the first flight of three aircraft dived to the starboard bow of the target, and dropped torpedoes. As the *Vittorio* turned to comb the tracks, she was caught abeam by the second flight of three aircraft.' The first sub-flight was led by Saunt in Albacore 4A, accompanied by 4C and 4F. They circled round to attack her from starboard, while the other sub-flight (5A, 4P and 4K), led by Lieutenant Arthur Abrams in 4K, made a tighter turn ahead of the turning battleship, and approached her from her port beam. This time the close-range Italian AA guns joined in, while her larger guns fired, too, creating a splash barrage – a line of shell splashes – intended to deter torpedo-bombers. As the torpedo-bombers approached, the two Fulmars dived in to strafe the battleship, in an attempt to distract the Italian gunners.

The Albacores all dived to 1,000 feet as they curved around to make their final approach. Meanwhile the Italian destroyers sped up to block the second group of aircraft which were approaching from the south, while the battleship herself turned hard to starboard, to throw off the aim of the first sub-flight. Having dropped down to around 100 feet, 4A and 4F of the first sub-flight dropped their torpedoes at a range of around 1,000 yards off the battleship's starboard beam, then banked away to the north. Meanwhile Sub-Lieutenant Richard Bradshaw in Albacore 4C, having been caught out by the battleship's hard turn, launched his torpedo 2,000 yards off the battleship's starboard bow. All three torpedoes, though, streaked past the battleship's stern. Hopkins later claimed that they had scored at least one torpedo hit, but he was mistaken.

Moments later the second sub-flight dropped down to make its torpedo run. All three planes dropped their torpedoes close to Bradshaw's, some 2,000 yards from the battleship. Two of these probably ran underneath the destroyers, but were too deep to hit them. All these torpedoes missed their target, too, passing astern of her. Having released their torpedoes, these three aircraft flew over their target, and headed off towards the north, after Saunt's sub-flight. All of the eight aircraft survived unscathed, and once out of range, they curved round to the east, and headed back towards *Formidable*.

They might have failed to hit the Italian battleship, but the attack had certainly made an impact. Admiral Iachino now knew that a British aircraft carrier was in the vicinity, and was most likely to the west of him. That meant it was likely that it was accompanied by Cunningham's battle fleet. The prudent course was to head away from this new threat, so Iachino ordered his force to break off its engagement with the British cruisers, and then turn away to the west-north-west, making 25 knots. He then ordered Sansonetti to do the same. The air strike had saved Pridham-Wippell's cruisers. It also, though, had now reduced the chances of Cunningham bringing the Italian flagship to battle. Thanks to all the smoke, Pridham-Wippell hadn't seen the air attack, and it was only due to a signal from *Gloucester* at 1138hrs that he knew what had happened. He ordered the smoke-laying to stop, and when it cleared, an empty horizon astern was revealed. Both the enemy battleship and the pursing heavy cruisers had gone.

By noon all three Italian forces were widely dispersed, but they were all heading across the Ionian Sea at full speed on a west-north-westerly course, in the direction of their base at Taranto. The Italian Force Y – the *Vittorio Veneto* and her escorts – was 48 miles to the south-west of Gavdos, and 40 miles away from the British cruisers, who now lay to the south-east. The two groups had steamed directly away from each other after the air attack, and it was noon before Pridham-Wippell felt safe enough to resume his pursuit of the Italians. The British battle fleet was roughly 65 miles to the east of Iachino's flagship,

Like its successor the Fairey Albacore, which had the advantage of an enclosed cockpit, the Fairey Swordfish torpedo-bomber had a three-man crew – the pilot, observer and telegraphist/rear gunner. Sometimes this third crewman, pictured here, was left behind, so his space could be used to stow an additional long-range fuel tank.

During the Matapan battle, the RAF in Greece used Bristol Blenheims to launch land-based air strikes against the Italian fleet. Their air crews, though, were not adequately trained in attacking naval targets, and their medium-level bombing attacks proved unsuccessful.

heading westwards as fast as Cunningham's ageing battleships would allow. Sansonetti's Force X was 22 miles to the south of Iachino, on a parallel course to the Italian flagship.

However, after turning away towards the north-west at 0915hrs, Cattaneo's Force Z hadn't been distracted by any brush with the British cruisers, and so had been able to steam at full speed. After two hours, at 1115hrs, his ships were 20 miles to the south-west of Gavdos. There, on Iachino's order, Cattaneo turned onto the same heading as the other Italian groups, and reduced speed slightly, so the three groups would be less scattered. By noon he was 55 miles west of Gavdos, and 50 miles to the north-west of Iachino. By noon Force Z was passing the longitude of 23° East, making it the most westerly of the three Italian groups, and therefore well out of range of *Formidable*'s aircraft. However, the other two groups were just an hour's flying time behind the British carrier, and both Cunningham and Boyd were keen to launch more air strikes, to slow the withdrawal of the Italian ships.

Still, it would take time to recover the first strike, and prepare a second. *Formidable* suffered slightly from having a relatively small air wing. That morning she had 27 aircraft embarked: 13 Fairey Fulmars, ten Fairey Albacores and four Fairey Swordfish. The last two were classed as torpedo-bomber/reconnaissance (TBR) aircraft, capable of functioning in either role. As well as forming or escorting offensive air strikes, these aircraft also had to perform a number of other vital duties, such as reconnaissance missions, anti-submarine patrolling and combat air patrol (CAP) – the airborne protection of the carrier herself. This, together with the number of aircraft requiring maintenance or repair, meant that any air strikes would rarely be larger than the one launched that morning. So, to boost his air power, Cunningham's staff had arranged with RAF Greece Command to provide aircraft capable of launching air strikes from the island, if suitable targets presented themselves.

The time for that had come when contact was made with the *Vittorio Veneto*. She was clearly the most important target in the area, unless more Italian capital ships were at sea. Almost as important were the two groups of Italian heavy cruisers and their escorts, forces X and Z. Now, though, all three Italian groups were speeding away from the airfields of Crete, and with their superior speed compared with Cunningham's battleships they were also drawing farther away from *Formidable*. So, Cunningham was keen to throw whatever aircraft he could into the attack, before the Italians drew completely out of range. Fortunately for him, while *Formidable*'s first air strike was returning to its carrier, a second strike was ranged on the carrier's flight deck, and was preparing to launch. It consisted of three Albacores and two Swordfish from 829 NAS, led by the squadron leader, Lieutenant-Commander John Dalyell-Stead. They were to be accompanied by two Fulmars from 803 NAS. At 1222hrs, after *Formidable* had turned into wind, these aircraft took off, and headed off in pursuit of Iachino's fleet.

THE GENERAL CHASE

The next air strike, though, wouldn't come from *Formidable*. Instead, the three torpedo-armed Swordfish that had taken off from Maleme in Crete a little over an hour before had been looking for the Italian fleet, and at noon they found them. The orders which had set them in motion had come from Cunningham's flagship at 0849hrs. The three aircraft of 815 NAS, originally embarked in *Illustrious*, had finally taken off two hours later at 1050hrs. The time lag was due in part to delays in forwarding the signal, and also because the aircraft had just returned from a dawn reconnaissance flight, and had to be refuelled. This meant that their target, Sansonetti's Force X, was no longer near the location given in their orders – the area where Sansonetti and Pridham-Wippell had first clashed. However, the three Swordfish led by Lieutenant Michael Torrens-Spence were updated on developments by *Formidable*, and so they flew on a south-south-westerly course at 9,000 feet, which by noon had taken them to a position some 30 miles to the west of the position cited in their orders.

At that altitude their search radius should have been 15–20 miles, but cloud cover and haze made visibility more patchy than expected. At noon they were rewarded by a sighting – three cruisers and four destroyers, on a heading of 300°, and making a little under 30 knots. It was Force X. When the sighting was made, the flight was just 7 miles to the west of the enemy, and therefore astern of them. Sansonetti's cruisers were in line ahead, with his flagship *Trento* in the lead, followed by *Trieste* and then *Bolzano*. The destroyers formed a screen half a mile ahead of the flagship. Torrens-Spence kept to the south of the Italians, using the sun as cover, while reducing altitude to 1,000 feet. At 1205hrs he gave the order to attack. The three Swordfish turned to starboard and dropped to around 100 feet before making their torpedo run. All of them dropped their torpedoes some 1,500 yards from the enemy, then banked hard away to the south.

The aircraft had been seen as they turned to make their approach. The Italian 10cm guns sent up a heavy AA barrage, reinforced by their close-range 40mm AA guns, while the 20.3cm main guns opened up, too, launching a splash barrage in the path of the low-flying Swordfish. This probably

The general chase, 0900–1200hrs, 28 March

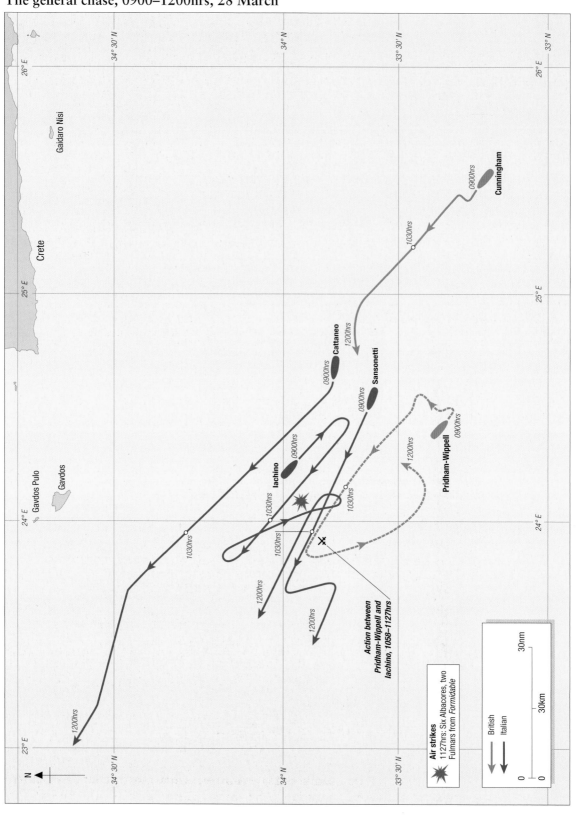

Gaidaro Nisi

Crete

Gavdos Pulo
Gavdos

Cunningham
0900hrs
1030hrs
1200hrs

Cattaneo
0900hrs
1200hrs

Sansonetti
0900hrs

Iachino
0900hrs

Pridham-Wippell
0900hrs
1200hrs

1030hrs
1030hrs
1030hrs
1030hrs

1200hrs
1200hrs
1200hrs

**Action between
Pridham-Wippell and
Iachino, 1058–1127hrs**

Air strikes
1127hrs: Six Albacores, two
Fulmars from *Formidable*

British
Italian

30nm
0   30km
0

N

encouraged the air crews to turn away sharply after dropping their torpedoes. The three cruisers reacted to the torpedoes by also turning sharply, with *Trieste* in the centre heading towards the torpedoes to comb them, while her consorts turned away. All three 18-inch torpedoes missed, with one passing astern of *Trieste*, and the others passing ahead and astern of *Bolzano*. None of the Swordfish were hit, and all three of them landed safely back at Maleme.

It was now clear that if any part of Iachino's fleet was to be brought to battle, then an Italian

warship would need to be damaged by an air strike. So, that became the priority that afternoon. At noon *Formidable* was detached from the battle fleet, accompanied by two destroyers. In this way, her frequent hauling off course to turn into wind for landing on or taking off wouldn't disrupt the rest of Cunningham's force. The carrier also had an edge in speed over Cunningham's three venerable battleships, and so the range between her and the Italians was less likely to increase as the afternoon wore on. This was, after all, now a pursuit (or a 'general chase' in naval parlance), as it had become clear that Iachino was heading back towards Taranto at full speed.

Shortly after noon the eight aircraft of the first strike had reached *Formidable*, and were 'stacked up' – flying in a holding pattern nearby while awaiting orders to land on. First, though, the carrier's second air strike had to be launched – five torpedo-bombers and two fighters. Also taking off was another Swordfish on a patrol mission. It was a busy time for the carrier, as a further two Fulmars, which had been flying air cover overhead, were due to land on, as was the Walrus floatplane from *Gloucester*, which had been unable to rejoin the cruiser. As soon as the second strike led by Lieutenant-Commander Dalyell-Stead took off, the other waiting aircraft landed on the carrier's flight deck. *Formidable* then turned back towards the rest of the battle fleet, which had forged ahead. Then, at 1232hrs, just as the flying operations were being completed, the alarm was sounded on board. A bomber had been spotted off the carrier's starboard bow, and it was approaching fast.

It had been flying too low to be picked up on radar, and was soon identified as an Italian SM.79 Sparviero torpedo-bomber. It was one of several Italian torpedo-bombers sent from Rhodes to search for the British fleet. The carrier was already making 30 knots, and when the bomber released its torpedo at a range of just 2,000m, Captain Bisset turned the carrier hard to port to avoid the torpedo. Meanwhile, *Formidable*'s AA guns opened up. A second SM.79 then appeared ahead of the carrier, and dropped its torpedo 1,500m away. Both torpedoes though, passed astern of the carrier. The Italian aircraft flew off unharmed, and *Formidable* resumed her original course, in pursuit of the Italian fleet. This, though, meant

During the 'general chase' phase of the Matapan operation, the ships of the British Mediterranean fleet were running at maximum speed for lengthy periods. This required engine room staff – such as these 'stokers' – to nurse their engines and propulsion systems, to make sure they worked as smoothly as possible.

In another grainy action shot, this photograph captures the moment when an Italian SM.79 torpedo-bomber dropped an aerial torpedo just 2,000m away from *Formidable*. Thanks to some deft shiphandling from Captain Bisset, though, the torpedo missed its mark. The photo, presumably taken by one of the carrier's ship's company, was published in a naval magazine.

that Iachino was now made aware of Cunningham's position. Thanks to delays in passing the reports on, it was 1425hrs before he learned that, two hours before, a reconnaissance flight from Rhodes had sighted 'a battleship, an aircraft carrier, and five destroyers'.

While *Formidable* had been conducting her flying operations, and then had come under attack, the battle fleet had continued on to the west, on a heading of 270°, and making 25 knots, with the slower *Barham* left to drop behind, escorted by a destroyer. That meant that with each hour that passed, the *Vittorio Veneto* would draw up to 5 miles ahead of them. Then, at 1230hrs, Pridham-Wippell's cruisers appeared in sight to the south-east, preceded by their destroyer screen. There had been no word from Pridham-Wippell for almost an hour after his encounter with the *Vittorio Veneto*, so this reunion had been unexpected. The cruiser commander, though, had been maintaining radio silence, and had steered a course he hoped would lead him towards Cunningham.

Until Pridham-Wippell was sighted, Cunningham and his men harboured a hope that they could still bring part of the enemy fleet to battle. The battleships even had their guns trained on a likely bearing off their starboard bow, while gun director crews and lookouts were eagerly hoping to be the first to spot the enemy. Cunningham hoped to make contact with Iachino at around 1330hrs, and spotter planes had even been launched from *Warspite*, in preparation for a surface gunnery action. Now, though, it became evident that a fleet action was not imminent. A frustrated Cunningham paced up and down his flagship's bridge 'like a caged tiger' in his eagerness to bring Iachino to battle. Confirmation from Pridham-Wippell that the Italians were definitely withdrawing put paid to the British admiral's hopes for a decisive gunnery action.

Cunningham's only solace was that with sunset at 1946hrs that evening, there were still over seven hours of daylight left. This meant there was still a chance that an air strike might be able to damage the enemy, and slow him down before nightfall. To increase the chance of this, Cunningham's staff had already asked the RAF for their help. As a result, Sunderland flying boats were dispatched from Greek airfields to conduct a search over the Ionian Sea. Even more useful, at Menidi, a Greek airfield some 20 miles north of Athens, some 24 Bristol Blenheim medium bombers were readied, drawn from 84, 113 and 211 squadrons. At 1235hrs, a Sunderland reported sighting an Italian battleship and four destroyers, 45 miles south-west of Gavdos. Within 15 minutes a strike of six Blenheims from 84 Squadron were in the air, and heading towards the target. A second strike of six bombers from 113 Squadron followed half an hour behind them, while two further strikes were prepared, but held in reserve.

These twin-engined bombers carried one 500lb (220kg) and two 250lb (110kg) bombs apiece, and so while not ideally suited for the task, they might cause enough superficial damage to the battleship to reduce her effectiveness.

The bombers climbed to 10,000 feet as they crossed over the Peloponnese, and then, to increase their chances of making contact, they split into two flights of three aircraft. That way they could cover as wide a swathe of sea as possible. At 1420hrs, the westernmost of the two flights sighted the *Vittorio Veneto* and her escorts, some 11 miles away to the south-west. They turned to attack the battleship from her starboard quarter, dropping to 4,000 feet as they approached. None of the nine bombs hit the battleship, and the attackers turned away. The second flight never made contact.

The second RAF strike by 113 Squadron sighted the battleship 20 minutes later at 1440hrs, and this time all six Blenheims were able to bomb her at 1450hrs. Again, all of the bombs missed, although the air crews claimed one possible hit. Iachino later recorded that the two bombing attempts were completely unsuccessful, which belies the airmen's claim. It was now almost 1500hrs. The 'General Chase' had been going on for 2½ hours now, and the Italians were clearly drawing away from Cunningham's battle fleet. Iachino's flagship was now 90 miles due west of Gavdos, while Sansonetti's force was on a parallel course to him, just within sight, some 15 miles to the south. Cunningham's battle fleet, though, was 80 miles astern of Iachino, his progress limited by *Barham*, which could only make 22 knots. The third Italian force, led by Cattaneo, was 50 miles to the north-west of Iachino, and 90 miles from Cunningham. So, given the widening range, the chance of a successful air strike was dwindling steadily as the afternoon wore on.

THE AFTERNOON AIR STRIKES

From Cunningham's perspective the situation was less than ideal. When his hopes of bringing about a surface action faded, he ordered Pridham-Wippell's cruiser force to move ahead of the battle fleet, and to form a scouting line, 16 miles ahead of *Warspite*. He learned of the failure of the three air attacks by aircraft operating from Crete and Greece, but was encouraged by the news that the RAF were launching two more strikes, both larger than the first ones. The stiff wind of the morning had also eased. This meant that *Formidable* would no longer have to break off to turn towards the north-east, to face into the wind for air operations. So, his battle fleet could remain together, and was able to make good progress. It was still a long way astern of Iachino, though, and everything now depended on *Formidable*'s air crews, or the RAF.

The air strike of five torpedo-bombers and two fighters which had been launched at 1230hrs had now been in the air for 2½ hours, and would be approaching the limit of its range and endurance. *Formidable* had been launching Fulmars to protect the carrier throughout the afternoon, and at 1400hrs three Albacores were launched, at Cunningham's request, to re-establish contact with Iachino and Sansonetti, after other British shadowing aircraft reported running low on fuel. These had flown in the earlier strike, but their Albacores were now used in a reconnaissance role. At 1459hrs, Lieutenant Michael Haworth, the observer in Albacore 4F, sighted the Italian battleship again, less than 10 minutes after the second Blenheim attack. So, Haworth and his pilot Lieutenant Henry Ellis were able to shadow the *Vittorio Veneto*, and send back regular reports on her movements. They continued to shadow the battleship until they were relieved shortly before sunset that evening.

The air strikes, 1200–1945hrs, 28 March

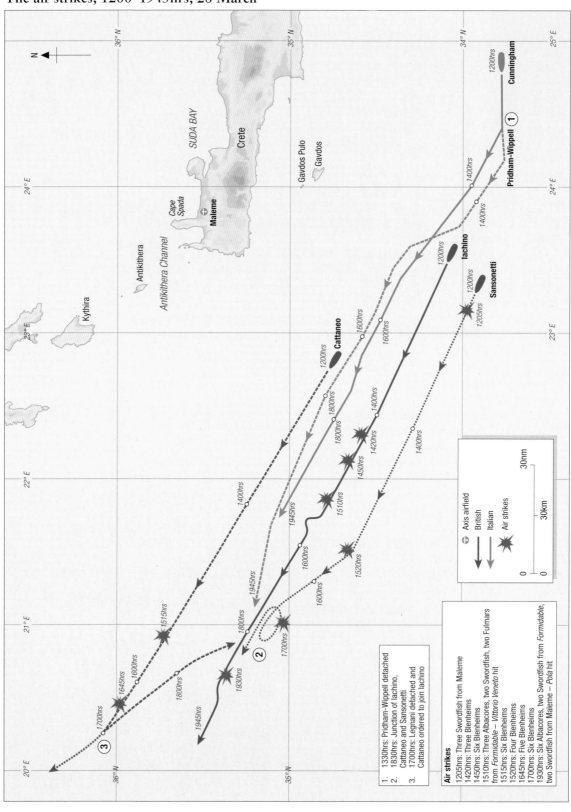

N

36° N

35° N

34° N

36° N

35° N

SUDA BAY

Crete

Cape Spada

Maleme

Antikithera Channel

Antikithera

Kythira

Gavdos Pulo

Gavdos

Cunningham
1200hrs

Pridham-Wippell ①

1400hrs

1400hrs

1400hrs

Iachino
1200hrs

Sansonetti
1200hrs

1205hrs

1600hrs

Cattaneo
1200hrs

1600hrs

1800hrs

1800hrs

1400hrs

1400hrs

1420hrs

1450hrs

1510hrs

1520hrs

1600hrs

1600hrs

1700hrs

1945hrs

1945hrs

1945hrs

1800hrs

1930hrs

②

1515hrs

1600hrs

1645hrs

1800hrs

1700hrs

③

20° E

21° E

22° E

23° E

24° E

25° E

1. 1330hrs: Pridham–Wippell detached
2. 1830hrs: Junction of Iachino, Cattaneo and Sansonetti
3. 1700hrs: Legnani detached and Cattaneo ordered to join Iachino

⊕ Axis airfield
British
Italian
✴ Air strikes

30nm

0

30km

0

Air strikes
1205hrs: Three Swordfish from Maleme
1420hrs: Three Blenheims
1450hrs: Six Blenheims
1510hrs: Three Albacores, two Swordfish, two Fulmars from *Formidable* – *Vittorio Veneto* hit
1515hrs: Six Blenheims
1520hrs: Four Blenheims
1645hrs: Five Blenheims
1700hrs: Six Blenheims
1930hrs: Six Albacores, two Swordfish from *Formidable*, two Swordfish from Maleme – *Pola* hit

52

Second (Afternoon) Strike – *Formidable*

Aircraft	Aircraft ID	Pilot	Observer	Telegraphist/Rear Gunner
Albacore	5G	Lieutenant-Commander Dalyell-Stead	Lieutenant Cooke	Petty Officer Blenkhorn
Albacore	5F	Lieutenant Whitworth	Sub-Lieutenant Ellis	Leading Airman Morris
Albacore	5H	Sub-Lieutenant Bibby	Sub-Lieutenant Parrish	Leading Airman Hogg
Swordfish	4B	Lieutenant Smith	unrecorded	unrecorded
Swordfish	5K	Lieutenant Osborn	Lieutenant Pain	Petty Officer Montague

Note: 5G was shot down during the strike, and all three of her crew were killed.

Then, at 1510hrs, *Formidable*'s second strike sighted the *Vittorio Veneto*. At the time she was steering 300°, and making 25 knots. Some 1,500 yards ahead of her were two Soldati-class destroyers. The strike was led by Lieutenant-Commander Dalyell-Stead, the commanding officer of 829 NAS, who flew one of his squadron's Albacores, 5G. He approached the battleship from the south-east, flying at 5,000 feet, and making good use of the sun. As he did so, he spotted Sansonetti's heavy cruisers and their escorts several miles away to the south-east. His five torpedo-bombers were divided into two sub-flights. The three Albacores (5F, 5G and 5H) were leading, followed by two Swordfish (4B and 5K), also from 829 NAS. Flying cover a little above and behind them were the two escorting Fulmars of 803 NAS. The aircraft worked their way 'up sun' and ahead of the battleship, then, when they were a little over a mile off her port beam, Dalyell-Stead gave the order to attack.

The tactics had already been decided. Essentially, they would be similar to those of the first strike. The torpedo-bombers would split up, and while the Albacores would attack their target from one side, the Swordfish would approach her from the opposite side. Meanwhile, the two fighters would swoop in to strafe the target ship, to distract her gunners. The Albacores passed ahead of the battleship before turning towards her, while behind them the Swordfish turned in a tighter circle, to attack her from the other beam. As they approached, they all dropped down to around 80 feet, ready for their torpedo run. It was a minute or so before they were spotted, but when they were, the battleship began turning hard to starboard, while ahead of her the two destroyers tried to turn beam-on to the approaching aircraft, so the full weight of the AA guns could bear. As the battleship turned, the three Albacores found themselves approaching her port side, but they still had to fly over the destroyers, which let loose a wall of AA fire.

Meanwhile, the two escorting Fulmars swooped in to strafe the battleship from 150 feet, attacking her from astern. Afterwards, they flew off unscathed towards the east. Seconds later the Albacores released their 18-inch Mark XII

Both the Albacore and the Swordfish carried a single 18-inch (45cm) Mark XII torpedo. Ideally, these had to be released while the torpedo-bomber was in level flight, with an airspeed below 60–70 knots, and at a height of less than 100 feet above the sea.

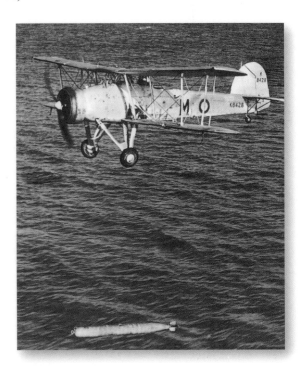

torpedoes 1,000 yards from the battleship's port side, and then tried to fly past her bows to make their escape towards the north. As she flew past, Dalyell-Stead's 5G was hit by close-range AA fire from the *Vittorio Veneto*, and she crashed into the sea, just 12 yards ahead of the battleship. All three of her crew were killed. Behind her, the other two Albacores, piloted by Lieutenant Alexander Whitworth and Sub-Lieutenant Robert Bibby both made it past her without being hit. At 1525hrs, as the last Albacores roared past her, the battleship was hit by a torpedo. It struck her in her port quarter, detonating beside her port outer propeller shaft. A tall plume of smoke and water erupted, rising as high as the battleship's funnel.

Meanwhile, the two Swordfish flown by lieutenants George Osborn and Kenneth Smith approached the turning battleship from what was now her starboard beam. As the battleship completed her turn onto a reciprocal easterly course, they both released their torpedoes simultaneously, at a range of just over 1,000 yards. The Swordfish then flew off past the battleship's stern, chased by AA fire from the destroyers. Later, in their after-action report, Osborn claimed they hadn't been fired on by the battleship before they released their torpedoes, which suggested remained undetected as they made their approach. Both torpedoes missed. However, that one hit, probably made by Dalyell-Stead's torpedo, had been a telling one. The detonation wrecked the *Vittorio Veneto*'s port outer propeller shaft, which forced that engine to be shut down. This immediately reduced the battleship's speed to just 15 knots. In all, 22 Italian crewmen were killed in the blast and its aftermath.

This meant that Cunningham's battle fleet, some 70 miles to the east and coming up at 22 knots, now had an outside chance of overhauling the *Vittorio Veneto* before nightfall. It altered things significantly. A moment before, the Italians were winning the race for the Italian coast, and the promise of land-based air cover from airfields in Apulia. Given its speed, the battleship should have been able to reach Taranto the following morning. Now, after the torpedo strike, it would be a full 24 hours before they reached port. Worse, Iachino now knew that somewhere to the east Cunningham was

Despite the poor quality of this grainy photograph, printed in a British wartime propaganda publication, this is a superb action image, showing Sansonetti's cruisers, with *Bolzano* at the rear, weaving to avoid bombs during an air attack from RAF Blenheims during the battle. The original photograph now appears to be lost.

approaching, with an aircraft carrier and at least one battleship. So, with sunset still more than four hours away, he could expect to be attacked by another air strike. The attacks by Beaufighters had demonstrated they were equally likely to be attacked by British bombers flying from Greece.

He was right about the threat posed by the RAF. As his flagship was being attacked, another group of British bombers was concentrating on Sansonetti's cruisers, some 15 miles away to the south-west. A little over an hour and a half before, at 1350hrs, four Blenheims of 84 Squadron had taken off from Menidi, followed 20 minutes later by six more from 211 Squadron This strike was aimed at Sansonetti's force. The last group was immediately followed by another five Blenheims from 84 Squadron, followed by a final group 25 minutes behind them of six Blenheims from 113 Squadron These two groups formed a strike which would target Cattaneo's cruisers. That meant that by 1430hrs a total of 21 Blenheims were heading out over the sea to attack Iachino's two cruiser divisions.

The first group to locate its target were the five bombers from 84 Squadron. At 1515hrs they came upon Cattaneo's force some 75 miles off the Peloponnese coast. The bombing run, though, didn't score any hits, although near misses were claimed on Cattaneo's flagship *Zara*. The second group of Blenheims from 113 Squadron didn't manage to spot the Italian ships until 1630hrs, having passed them to the east. However, they attacked at 1645hrs, and again, while no hits were achieved, the air crews claimed a near miss by a 500lb bomb on the light cruiser *Giuseppe Garibaldi*.

Approximately 50 miles away to the south, and within sight of the *Vittorio Veneto*, Sansonetti's division was under attack from the other group of Blenheims. At 1520hrs, as *Formidable*'s air strike was approaching the *Vittorio Veneto*, some 12 miles to the south-south-east the remaining four Blenheims of 84 Squadron sighted Sansonetti's force, and began their bombing run. This time they claimed two hits with 250lb bombs on one heavy cruiser, and a single hit by a 500lb bomb on another. In fact, the bombs had narrowly missed the *Trento* and *Trieste*, and no hits were achieved. After a lengthy pause, just before 1700hrs, the last group of six Blenheims from 211 Squadron arrived, and dropped their bombs over Sansonetti's cruisers, but none of these hit anything. Surprisingly, in all of these attacks on the Italian cruisers, none of the bombers were hit by AA fire, which the airmen reported had been extremely heavy.

Meanwhile, ever since the torpedo hit on the Italian flagship, her damage control teams had been hard at work trying to stop the flooding in the battleship's stern compartments, and counter-flooding other compartments to restore her trim. In all, some 3,500 tons of water had entered the battleship,

The Italian light cruiser *Abruzzi* was the flagship of Rear Admiral Antonio Legnani, commander of the 8th Cruiser Division. Although attached to Cattaneo's command during the battle, the *Abruzzi* and her sister ship *Giuseppe Garibaldi* were detached and ordered to return to Brindisi.

AIR STRIKE ON THE ITALIAN FLAGSHIP, 1525HRS (PP. 56–57)

After being attacked by British naval aircraft that forenoon, the Italian flagship *Vittorio Veneto* had been steaming away from the British, heading towards the Italian coast. For a while the British had lost contact with her, but search aircraft had been looking for her, and in mid-afternoon she was re-located. A second air strike was duly launched from *Formidable*, and at 1510hrs it sighted the battleship 70 miles to the south-west of Crete. The strike's leader, Lieutenant-Commander Dalyell-Stead, gave the order to attack. His small force consisted of three Albacore and two Swordish torpedo-bombers, escorted by two Fulmar fighters.

When the aircraft were spotted, the Italian battleship began a tight turn to starboard, to steam on a reciprocal course. The attackers split up, with Dalyell-Stead attempting to attack the battleship from port with the Albacores, while the Swordfish attacked her from starboard. The Albacores were first to attack, dropping down from 5,000ft before beginning their torpedo runs. Dalyell-Stead in Albacore 5G (**1**) was the first to release his torpedo, at a range of 1,000 yards. Then, Albacores 5H and5F (**2a** and **2b**) did the same. Climbing away wasn't a real option, as the

torpedo-bombers were too slow, so the first tried to cross the battleship's bow before escaping. However, 5G was hit by close-range machine-gun fire, and crashed into the sea just yards ahead of the battleship (**3**). Their torpedoes were already in the water, though, and at 1525hrs one of the torpedoes, probably the one from 5F, struck the battleship's stern, wrecking her outer port propeller (**4**).

Meanwhile, the two Swordfish 4B and 5K (**5** and **6**) were approaching the battleship from the south, and were dropping down to carry out their own torpedo runs from off the *Vittorio Veneto*'s starboard beam. To distract the battleship's gunners, the two Fulmars L and M carried out strafing runs over the *Vittorio Veneto* during each of the attacks, raking her decks with their machine guns as they swept over her.

The whole attack lasted less than six minutes. Only one aircraft, Dalyell-Stead's Albacore, was lost, with all of her three-man crew, but the *Vittorio Veneto* suffered at least 22 casualties, and the damage to her propeller meant that her speed was now reduced to just 15 knots. This meant the British battle fleet now had a chance to overhaul her before dark.

which was now noticeably down by the stern. Although the real damage to the *Vittorio Veneto* had been limited to her outer port shaft, both of her port propellers had to be stopped while the flooding was dealt with and attempts were made to determine the extent of the damage to the outer shaft. The battleship's auxiliary rudders had also been damaged, which made steering more problematic. Ironically, the flooding had also put the after pump room out of action, and so it took time to bring portable pumping equipment into action from the second pumping station farther forward. So, until 1600hrs she was only able to limp along at a little over 10 knots, using her starboard shafts. It was 1700hrs before her inner port shaft was back in operation, and she was finally able to proceed at 15 knots.

By 1700hrs, Iachino had reached a decision. After these air attacks, and with more expected before nightfall, he decided to concentrate his forces around his damaged flagship. This was a sensible solution to his problem, as it meant the *Vittorio Veneto* would then be afforded the best possible protection against further air attacks. There was another even more compelling reason for this concentration of force. Reconnaissance reports suggested that Cunningham was about 65 miles away to the east, which equated to three hours of steaming. That meant that even with the *Vittorio Veneto* able to proceed at half speed, Cunningham might well be able to reach him during the night. Worse still was the even more real threat that Cunningham might detach his destroyers and send them forging ahead to attack him out of the darkness.

So, Iachino ordered Sansonetti to join him with his whole force of three heavy cruisers and three destroyers. To the north, Cattaneo was ordered to detach his light cruisers *Abruzzi* and *Giuseppe Garibaldi*, and send them ahead to Brindisi, together with the force's destroyers as an escort. The remains of Cattaneo's force – three heavy cruisers – would join the rest of the fleet by 1830hrs. Then, when sunset came 76 minutes later, the damaged battleship would be surrounded by a powerful ring of cruisers and destroyers. That should be proof enough against any night-time destroyer attack. It was exactly the right thing to do, given the circumstances.

Shortly after 1700hrs, after brushing off the second of two attacks by land-based British bombers, Cattaneo was ordered to turn his force around. He was now to head off back towards the south-east, to rendezvous with Iachino. After detaching his light cruisers, Cattaneo led the heavy cruisers *Zara*, *Fiume* and *Pola* away from the safety of the Italian coast, and set a course towards the *Vittorio Veneto*, which was then about 70 miles away to the east-south-east. That meant that if the flagship remained on course, and if Cattaneo maintained his speed, the two groups would rendezvous about 20 miles from Iachino's current position, at around 1830hrs that evening. That gave Iachino and his captains a little over an hour to rearrange the fleet before sunset. Darkness, of course, would bring an end to the threat posed by British aircraft.

Iachino was still unsure where Cunningham or Pridham-Wippell were, and the reports of land-based search aircraft operating from Rhodes had been both confusing and contradictory. He had been reluctant to launch his own

Rear Admiral Legnani commanded the 8th Cruiser Division at Matapan. He was the only senior Italian commander who didn't play an active role in the battle.

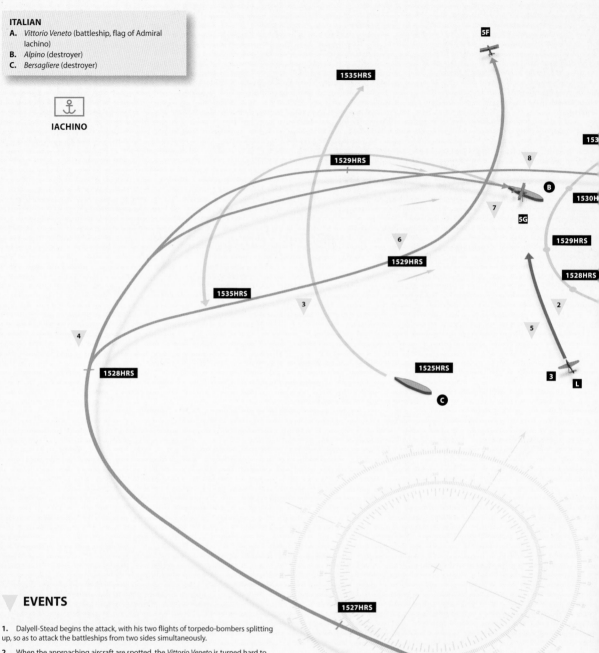

ITALIAN
A. *Vittorio Veneto* (battleship, flag of Admiral Iachino)
B. *Alpino* (destroyer)
C. *Bersagliere* (destroyer)

IACHINO

5F

1535HRS

1529HRS

8

153

1530H

B

7

5G

1529HRS

6

1528HRS

1529HRS

1525HRS

2

3

5

1535HRS

3

4

1528HRS

L

C

1527HRS

EVENTS

1. Dalyell-Stead begins the attack, with his two flights of torpedo-bombers splitting up, so as to attack the battleships from two sides simultaneously.

2. When the approaching aircraft are spotted, the *Vittorio Veneto* is turned hard to starboard, and opens fire with her AA guns.

3. The two escorting destroyers turn beam-on to the approaching aircraft, and begin firing too, concentrating on the Albacores, which pass over them to reach the battleship.

4. At 1528hrs the Alabacores split up to throw off the enemy gunners, and approach the battleship from different angles. By now they have dropped down to just 100ft.

5. To draw fire from the Albacores, a Fulmar strafes the battleship from stern to bow, then flies off towards the north.

6. At 1529hrs the three Albacores drop their torpedoes at a range of around 1,000 yards from the target, which by this stage is presenting her port beam to them.

7. Dalyell-Stead in 5G is hit by AA fire, and his Albacore crashes into the sea directly in front of the battleship. There are no survivors.

8. His torpedo, though, strikes the *Vittorio Veneto*'s stern at 1530hrs, severely damaging her outer port-side propeller shaft, and damaging her port rudder. The battleship, still turning, immediately begins to lose speed. The other two torpedoes miss the battleship.

9. Having approached from the south, at 1531hrs the two Swordfish release their torpedoes 1,000 yards from the starboard beam of the battleship. The torpedoes pass astern of their target.

10. Meanwhile, the remaining Fulmar strafes the battleship from bow to stern, before flying away to the south.

11. The remaining British aircraft escape towards the north, before forming up out of range, and returning to *Formidable*.

0

1

NAUTICAL MILE

THE SECOND AIR STRIKE ON THE *VITTORIO VENETO*, 1525–1540HRS, 28 MARCH

The second air strike of the day launched from the aircraft carrier *Formidable* consisted of five torpedo-bombers and two escorting fighters, and was led by Lieutenant-Commander Dalyell-Stead, who piloted the Albacore 5G. They sighted the battleship *Vittorio Veneto* at 1510hrs, while approaching from the east at 8,000ft. Over the next 15 minutes they approached unobserved, working their way into a position where they could attack out of the sun. At the same time, the aircraft dropped down to 5,000ft. So far they were unobserved. Then, when Dalyell-Stead gave the order to attack, the 1st Sub-flight of Albacores curved round to the west and north to attack the battleship from one beam, while the 2nd Sub-flight of Swordfish planned to attack her from the opposite side. Meanwhile, the battleship and its two escorting destroyers opened up with a furious barrage of anti-aircraft fire.

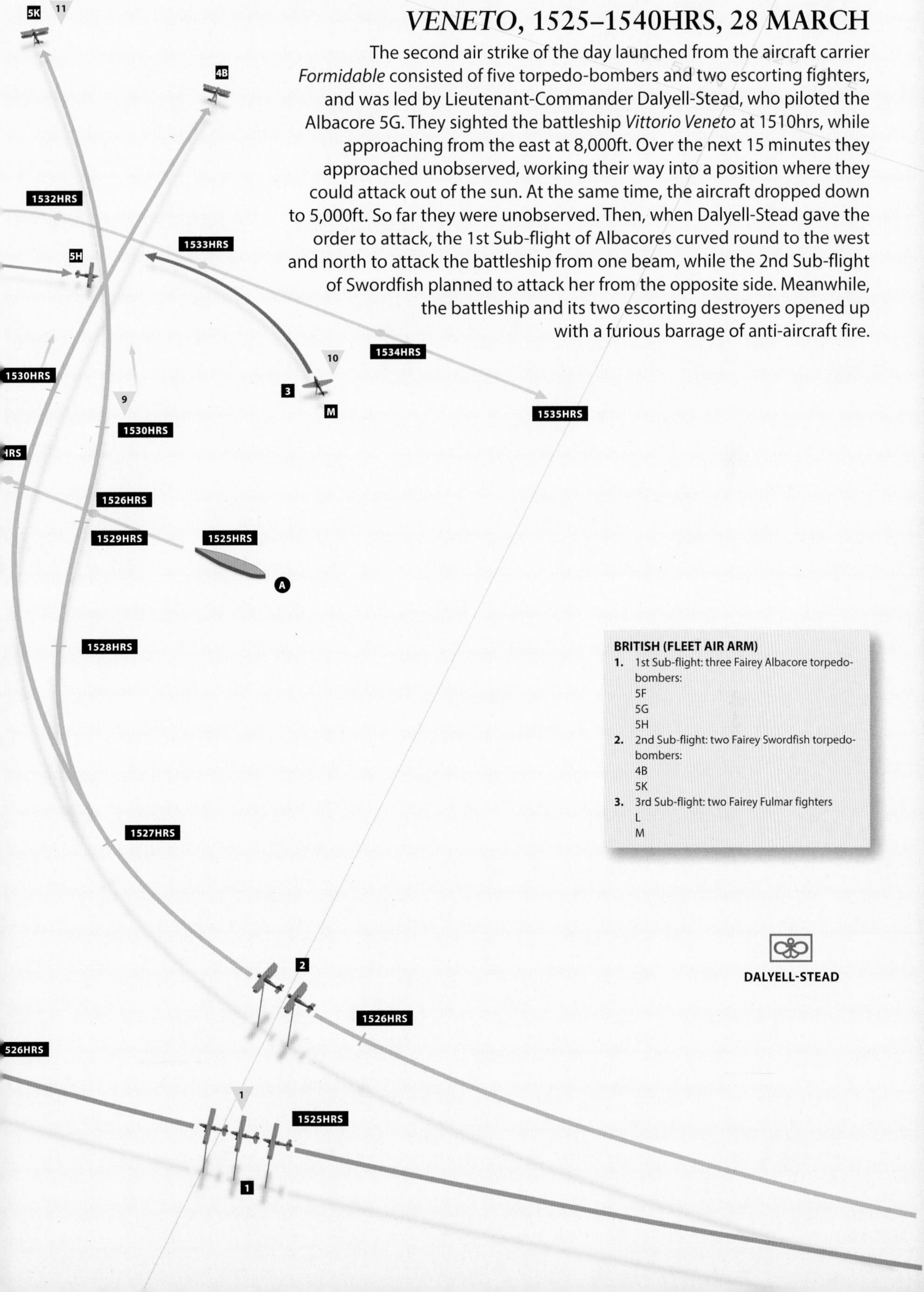

5K
11
4B
1532HRS
1533HRS
5H
1530HRS
10
1534HRS
3
M
1535HRS
9
1530HRS
1526HRS
1529HRS
1525HRS
A
1528HRS
1527HRS
2
1526HRS
526HRS
1
1526HRS
1
1525HRS

BRITISH (FLEET AIR ARM)
1. 1st Sub-flight: three Fairey Albacore torpedo-bombers:
   5F
   5G
   5H
2. 2nd Sub-flight: two Fairey Swordfish torpedo-bombers:
   4B
   5K
3. 3rd Sub-flight: two Fairey Fulmar fighters
   L
   M

DALYELL-STEAD

floatplanes, carried on his flagship and in his cruisers, as recovering them would delay the fleet's progress towards the Italian coast. His best guess during the late afternoon was that Cunningham's battle fleet, with a strength of at least two or three capital ships, including *Formidable*, was about 80 miles astern of him. So, now that the *Vittorio Veneto* was under way again, albeit at half speed, it was unlikely that Cunningham would catch up with him before nightfall. There remained the risk, though, that his British opponent would send his faster light cruisers and destroyers ahead of him to stage a night attack. If the fleet was spared any air attacks before dark, that would then be the greatest threat he faced.

His anxiety would have increased markedly if Iachino had known that the British were closer than he'd imagined. At 1700hrs, the British battle fleet was about 55 miles astern of him, and although it was making just 22 knots thanks to *Barham*, it was still gaining on the *Vittorio Veneto* at a relative speed of 7 miles an hour. Thanks to intermittent sighting reports of the *Vittorio Veneto* that afternoon, Cunningham knew that the Italian battleship had heaved to after the last of *Formidable*'s air attacks. One of these came from Lieutenant-Commander Bolt, the fleet observer, in the flagship's own Swordfish floatplane. He had been catapulted off *Warspite* at 1215hrs, with the task of acting as a visual link between the British forces at sea, and to keep Cunningham appraised of the changing tactical situation. This, of course, also included shadowing the enemy. Bolt remained airborne until almost 1700hrs, at which point he had to return to *Warspite*.

By then the *Vittorio Veneto* had got under way again, limping away towards the north-west. As Bolt had lingered too long to return to Maleme to refuel, he had no option but to return to *Warspite*. In theory, this meant the battleship had to break off pursuit to hoist the Swordfish floatplane back on board. However, in a risky but impressive manoeuvre, the aircraft was recovered safely, even though *Warspite* had only reduced speed to 18 knots. For much of the afternoon, Bolt had been Cunningham's most reliable 'eyes and ears'. So, after reporting to the Admiralty, Cunningham ordered Bolt back into the air, to relocate Iachino's flagship, and to keep sending back his impeccably accurate sighting reports. Cunningham estimated that it would take 6 hours to come within gun range of Iachino's flagship, which meant they could overhaul her before midnight. Cunningham was confident he could overpower the enemy battleship in a night action. That was something his Mediterranean Fleet had trained for, and would excel in.

As Iachino had feared, Cunningham had also ordered Pridham-Wippell to range ahead of the battle fleet, in an attempt to delay the Italians long enough for Cunningham to catch them up. The light cruisers *Ajax*, *Gloucester*, *Orion* and *Perth* were detached at 1644hrs, and headed off at 30 knots. They had already been deployed 16 miles ahead of the battle fleet, and so, to maintain visual contact between the two groups, Cunningham also detached the destroyers *Nubian* and *Mohawk*, to take station between the two forces. By this stage Cunningham was unsure where one of the two Italian cruiser groups was. Delays and innacuracies in reports from the RAF in Greece didn't help him build up an accurate picture. However, he was aware that in general terms, Sansonetti was to the south of the *Vittorio Veneto*, as he had been sighted on the south-western horizon by his flagship's own Walrus. It

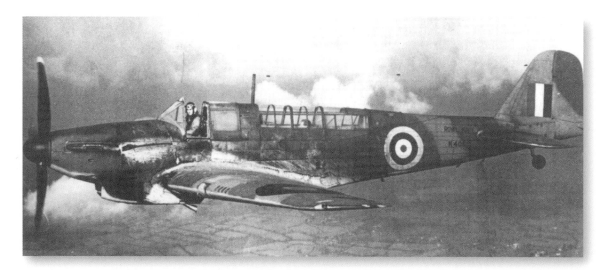

was Cattaneo's location that concerned him, as he could potentially pose a threat to Pridham-Wippell.

So, at the same time as he detached Pridham-Wippell, Cunningham had ordered Boyd on *Formidable* to prepare another air strike. With sunset less than three hours away, it was clear that any such air strike would be the last one of the day, unless he was willing to place his aircraft at risk in attempting a night landing. By late afternoon, Cunningham had two rolls of the dice. The first was the air strike, which would target the crippled battleship in an attempt to prevent her from escaping. His second was Pridham-Wippell, whose light cruisers could be expected to reach the Italians at around sunset, 1946hrs. Cunningham hoped his deputy would be able to use his superior speed and manoeuvrability to harry Iachino with guns and torpedoes. With luck, he could inflict enough damage to slow him down. This, though, was extremely risky, as Pridham-Wippell would be heavily outnumbered and outgunned. It would fully test the night-fighting abilities of his crews.

For air defence *Formidable* carried the Fairey Fulmar, a large two-seater fighter. While it wasn't particularly manoeuvrable or speedy, it was robust, and could absorb damage. During the Matapan air strikes, covering Fulmars strafed the target, to distract its AA gunners.

THE DUSK STRIKE

That done, as *Formidable* prepared her third air strike, Cunningham and his staff prepared the rest of the fleet for a night battle. His orders to Pridham-Wippell had been explicit: 'If cruisers gain touch with damaged battleship, 2nd and 14th Destroyer Flotillas will be sent to attack. If she is not then destroyed, battle fleet will follow in.' He added a postscript, in case Pridham-Wippell failed to make contact with the *Vittorio Veneto*: 'If not located by cruisers, I intend to work round to the north and then west, and regain touch in the morning.' Then, between 1740hrs and 1750hrs, *Formidable* launched her final air strike of the day. It consisted of six Albacores and two Swordfish, under the command of Lieutenant-Commander Saunt, who was flying Albacore 4A. All but one of them had taken part in the earlier strikes – four in the forenoon and three that afternoon. The exception was Swordfish 4H, piloted by Sub-Lieutenant Thorpe, who was on his first strike, as his aircraft had been flying reconnaissance missions earlier in the day. After forming up, they set off towards the north-west, making around 60 knots.

Third (Dusk) Strike – *Formidable*

Aircraft type	Aircraft ID	Pilot	Observer	Telegraphist/Rear Gunner
Albacore	4A	Lieutenant-Commander Saunt	Lieutenant Hopkins	–
Albacore	4K	Lieutenant Abrams	Lieutenant Smith-Shand	–
Albacore	4P	Sub-Lieutenant Tuke	Sub-Lieutenant Wilson	–
Albacore	5A	Sub-Lieutenant Williams	Midshipman Davis	Leading Airman Booth
Albacore	5F	Lieutenant Whitworth	Sub-Lieutenant Ellis	Leading Airman Morris
Albacore	5H	Sub-Lieutenant Bibby	Sub-Lieutenant Parrish	Leading Airman Hogg
Swordfish	4H	Sub-Lieutenant Thorpe	Lieutenant Rushworth-Lund	Airman Japp
Swordfish	5K	Lieutenant Osborn	Lieutenant Pain	Pilot Office Montague

Note: 4A, 4K and 4P had no third crewman as they were fitted with long-range tanks instead.

At 1745hrs, as the strike took off, *Warspite*'s Swordfish floatplane was also catapulted from the flagship, and she too headed off towards the *Vittorio Veneto*. Again, Lieutenant-Commander Bolt would act as Cunningham's eyes before it became too dark to see. At 1831hrs, two hours before the end of twilight, Bolt radioed in the first of a string of highly accurate reports on both the course and speed of the enemy fleet, and on the air strike that followed. His first report gave the position of the *Vittorio Veneto*, and reported that she was under way, and making around 12–15 knots. In fact, according to Iachino, his flagship had, by then, managed to coax 16 knots out of her remaining engines. More importantly, Bolt reported that the battleship and her escorts had now been joined by Sansonetti's three cruisers, and their escorting destroyers, which had formed up in two columns on the port side of the flagship. *Vittorio Veneto*'s own destroyers were in a similar column to starboard. Bolt also estimated that the *Vittorio Veneto* was now approximately 55 miles away from Cunningham.

The second Italian cruiser force, led by Cattaneo, had separated into two groups at 1700hrs, and as the two light cruisers continued on to Brindisi, with a destroyer escort, the cruisers *Zara*, *Pola* and *Fiume* had turned towards the south-east, steaming at high speed to their rendezvous with the crippled *Vittorio Veneto*. When Bolt began his reporting, they were spotted several miles away, and were now approaching Iachino's combined force from the north-west. It would take time for them to take station around the flagship, but to Bolt it was clear that this concentration of force would be completed before 1930hrs. When it happened, Cattaneo's cruisers took station in a column on the

The cramped cockpit of a Fairey Swordfish was open, which may have been uncomfortable, but, according to air crews it afforded the pilot a better view during a torpedo attack. The observer sat directly behind the pilot.

starboard side of the flagship, with a line of destroyers in another column to starboard.

That meant that the Italian fleet was now arrayed in five parallel columns. In the centre was the *Vittorio Veneto*, with two destroyers ahead of her, and two more astern. On either side of her, 1,200m away, was a column of three heavy cruisers – *Trento*, *Trieste* and *Bolzano* to port, and *Zara*, *Pola* and *Fiume* to starboard. Beyond the cruisers, 1,000m off on either beam, was a column of destroyers – three on the port side of the fleet, and four on the starboard side. This whole armada of 18 warships was now heading towards the north-west, on a course of 300°, and making 16 knots. Essentially, Iachino had thrown a steel ring around his crippled flagship. If they were attacked by another air strike, or even if Cunningham launched a destroyer attack during the night, the flagship would be well protected.

When the air strike from *Formidable* drew close to this powerful Italian fleet, Saunt decided to hold back, waiting for the light to fade before launching his attack. Instead, he held his aircraft in a holding area just out of sight to the west. Even when carrying a torpedo, his biplanes had an endurance of five hours. The three Albacores carrying long-range tanks in lieu of a telegraphist/rear gunner could remain airborne for up to nine hours. So, Saunt bided his time, and waited for dark. Meanwhile, below him, Pridham-Wippell's four light cruisers had been steaming towards the west-north-west, and passed beneath the aircraft on their way to regain contact with the Italians. At 1918hrs lookouts on *Orion* spotted the enemy fleet off the cruiser's port beam, at a range of just 10 miles. It was still over half an hour until sunset, but visibility was already deteriorating, aided slightly by a haze on the water. Pridham-Wippell's orders, though, were to shadow the enemy, rather than attack them.

Instead, Cunningham planned to use his destroyers to strike at the enemy, if the final air strike didn't achieve anything. This would be carried out by two destroyer flotillas. Captain Philip Mack's 14th Flotilla consisted of Mack's own *Janus*, as well as *Nubian* and *Mohawk*. These two Tribal-class destroyers had been detached earlier, to act as a visual link between Cunningham and Pridham-Wippell. At sunset they would rejoin *Janus* off the port bow of the battle fleet. Off Cunningham's starboard bow was the 2nd Flotilla, under the command of Captain Hugh St. Lawrence Nicolson. He commanded four destroyers: his own *Ilex*, together with *Hasty*, *Hereward* and *Hotspur*. When ordered to launch a torpedo attack, these two flotillas would surge forward, and would attack the enemy as directed by Pridham-Wippell, who had them under observation. A third group of destroyers, the 10th Flotilla, commanded by Captain Hector Waller, would remain with the battle fleet, serving as a screen. Waller's flotilla was made up of the destroyers *Stuart*, *Griffin*, *Greyhound* and *Havock*.

When Pridham-Wippell judged the time to be right, Cunningham would release Mack and Nicolson's flotillas, and they would race forward before attacking the Italian fleet from the north-east, from the fleet's starboard quarter. That way the destroyers would be hard to see in the fading light, while the Italians ships would be silhouetted. Much, though, depended on knowing exactly where the enemy fleet was, and what it was doing. This largely depended on Bolt, in his shadowing Swordfish. Later, Bolt recalled how it all worked:

We carried out our reconnaissance duties and passed our reports by W/T [wireless transmitter] direct to Alexandria W/T station, at a distance of some 400 miles. We had carried out a great deal of practice with this station during dawn anti-submarine patrols from Alexandria, and it was very satisfying that PO Pace, my telegraphist air-gunner, was able to clear some dozen 'Operational Immediate' messages in a matter of minutes. These signals repeated by Alexandria W/T to Malta and Gibralter were recieved immediately in Whitehall W/T, and the Admiralty had them nearly as soon as the Commander-in-Chief in *Warspite*.

He first caught sight of the *Vittorio Veneto* at 1820hrs, and shortly afterwards he began his string of signals. This told Cunningham the enemy had formed up into a defensive formation, and were still 50 miles ahead of him. That still meant it would be four hours before the enemy were within gun range. By then, Bolt would have lost contact in the dark, and the chances were Iachino would slip away in the night. So, while the impending air strike was still important, Cunningham reckoned that his best chance to stop the enemy lay with his destroyers.

Sunset was at 1946hrs that evening, but nautical twilight would last for another hour, as the sun's rays gradually faded into a violet glow on the western horizon. The start of that sunset was what Lieutenant-Commander Saunt was waiting for. His delay in launching the attack was providential, as late that afternoon, two Swordfish from 815 NAS had taken off from Maleme, and although they were officially flying west to augment Cunningham's search capability, they also carried torpedoes – the last ones available in the whole of Crete. The two Swordfish were guided by a sighting

A Tribal-class destroyer under way. When these first entered service they were described as 'gun destroyers', because their torpedo armament was limited to just one quadruple launcher, but they carried eight 4.7-inch guns apiece. The Tribals *Mohawk* and *Nubian* took part in the battle.

report from a Maleme-based Fulmar, and so, Lieutenant Torrens-Spence, the commander of 815 NAS, decided to fly almost due west.

The Italian fleet was approximately 140 miles from Maleme, which would have put the aircraft at the limit of their range and endurance. So, to make them more flexible, the telegraphist/rear gunner was left behind, to make room for a long-range tank. After 140 minutes in the air, at 1810hrs they sighted the Italian fleet, 25 miles ahead of them. Torrens-Spence had the same idea as Saunt – to wait until sunset before launching an attack. At 1835hrs, though, they spotted Saunt's air strike, and flew over to it and joined the other aircraft. That gave Saunt a slightly more potent force of six Albacores and four Swordfish.

(Dusk) Strike Maleme 815 NAS

Aircraft	Pilot	Observer	Telegraphist/Rear Gunner
Swordfish	Lieutenant Torrens-Spence	Sub-Lieutenant Winter	–
Swordfish	Lieutenant Kiggell	Sub-Lieutenant Bailey	–

Note: Both aircraft had no third crewman as they were fitted with long-range tanks instead.

At 1915hrs, some 20 minutes after his reinforcements had arrived, Saunt judged it was time to launch the air strike. The glow of the setting sun had now almost faded, leaving only a greyness in the western sky. In those light conditions there was a good chance that his aircraft wouldn't be spotted if they approached from the east. It also meant the Italian warships would be silhouetted, and so easier to make out. The Italian fleet was waiting for them, though, as Iachino fully expected an air attack before the moonless night rendered it impossible. So, all of his ships were at action stations, all ships running without showing any lights, and with air and surface lookouts at full readiness.

Iachino had already issued standing orders, covering what the fleet should do in the event of an air attack. All ships would make smoke, and stand ready for changes of course, on the orders of the flagship. The destroyers in the outer columns would also switch on their searchlights, in an attempt to dazzle the pilots as they made their approach. As the light faded, Iachino and his men began to think that a last-minute air strike wasn't coming.

By then, though, it was already under way. Saunt had split his forces, so they would attack the fleet from both port and starboard quarters at the same time. At 1915hrs, just as the British torpedo-bombers were labouring into position, Iachino ordered his fleet to alter course to port, from a heading of 300° to 270°. Their speed remained the same. So, instead of approaching directly onto the beam of the fleet, the attackers were now approaching it from slightly farther ahead, which made the aircraft somewhat easier to spot. That night the Italian lookouts did their job well. At 1928hrs a lookout on the destroyer *Alpino*, at the rear of the fleet's central column, spotted approaching aircraft, and raised the alarm.

The peace of the evening was shattered as the larger ships opened up, putting up a heavy AA barrage to either side of the fleet, while the destroyers' searchlights began probing the sea and sky around them. Oily black smoke began to pour from the warships' funnels, together with white smoke from smoke generators. Iachino ordered an immediate course change, back onto a heading of 300°. The attackers were 3,000 yards from the Italian fleet when the ships opened fire, described as 'a tremendous barrage of flaming onions [flak bursts] and shells from AA and other guns'. To the airmen, it appeared to be launched in all directions, without much central control. By then, though, the torpedo-bombers had dropped down to below 100 feet, and so much of this curtain of fire was directed above them.

Saunt's observer, Lieutenant Frank Hopkins recounted the scene:

> When we eventually went in to attack from the dark side, with the Italians silhouetted against the last glow of light to the west, we found that we had been spotted at long range, and were met with an impassable barrage of fire. We were forced to withdraw, and split up and came in again, individually, from different angles. The barrage of fire put up by the Italians was immensely spectacular but not very effective. A good deal of hose-piping [wild, unaimed firing] went on which resulted in a number of their ships hitting each other, but little damage to our own aircraft.

Hopkins may have sounded casual, but it took a special kind of courage to carry out a torpedo attack in a lumbering biplane, into the teeth of heavy fire.

The primary target was the *Vittorio Veneto*, but she was well protected by the ring of warships. So, most of the attackers released their torpedoes outside the protective ring, and had to hope for a lucky hit on her. At least three torpedo-bombers launched their torpedoes off the port beam of the fleet, and as the torpedoes were set deep they would run under the outer line of destroyers, to hit one of the larger targets beyond them. In any case, with all the wild AA fire, funnel smoke and waving searchlight beams, it was almost impossible to make out the battleship. These torpedoes were dropped about 200–500 yards from the destroyers, and so around 2,500 yards from the *Vittorio Veneto*. Scoring a hit was unlikely. In the end, all of these torpedoes missed the Italian ships. So, too, did the torpedo dropped by Sub-Lieutenant Anthony 'Steady' Tuke of Albacore 4P off the fleet's port beam, which narrowly passed astern of the battleship.

Similarly, Sub-Lieutenant Bibby flying Albacore 5H approached the fleet from its port quarter, and his torpedo passed astern of the *Fiume*, narrowly

This remarkable photograph, taken during the third air strike by aircraft from *Formidable*, shows an Albacore attempting to climb over the bows of the *Pola* after dropping her torpedo. The picture was taken through the struts of a Swordfish.

close by the battleship. It looked like Iachino's defensive ring was working. At the same time, Lieutenant Launcelot Kiggell from Maleme's 815 NAS passed ahead of the line of destroyers in the fleet's port column, and released his torpedo as he drew level with the cruiser *Trento*, which was leading the fleet's inner port column. He reported afterwards that he never actually saw much of the Italian fleet, due to all the smoke. The torpedo, though, with just 1,250 yards to run, passed ahead of the battleship. As the attackers had split up to attack from different directions, the torpedo runs were all made at different times. In some ways this made it safer, as it took a few seconds for the aircraft to be spotted, and fire switched to it. It also increased the wildness of the AA fire, which now seemed to be firing randomly in all directions.

This unplanned staggering of the attacks also meant that the air strike lasted longer than Saunt had planned. One of the last of the attackers was Sub-Lieutenant Grainger Williams, flying Albacore 5A. He approached from the starboard beam of the fleet at 1945hrs, just as the sun finally disappeared over the horizon. Like Kiggell, he had flown as far as the destroyer screen before releasing his torpedo towards the centre of the Italian fleet. He banked away as he flew over the line of Cattaneo's three cruisers. As he did, at 1946hrs, the central one, *Pola*, was hit amidships on her starboard side. An immense column of water erupted, but Williams and his observer never saw it, on account of the mass of black and white funnel smoke coming from the cruisers.

One of the last attacks was by Lieutenant Torrens-Spence of 815 NAS. He tried to climb above the fleet to get a better view, then dropped down behind the starboard column of Italian cruisers. He released his torpedo at 1950hrs close to the starboard bow of the *Fiume*, the rearmost cruiser. His target was the battleship some 1,200 yards ahead, but the torepdo missed its target. Torrens-Spence's Swordfish was hit as he turned away, but the damage wasn't fatal. That, surprisingly, was the only hit to any of the attacking aircraft. At sea level, though, the cruiser *Pola* was in trouble. The 18-inch torpedo had detonated between the cruiser's starboard boiler and engine rooms, causing extensive flooding. She quickly lost power and slowed to a halt. Amid all the smoke, the firing and the excitement, the other ships in the fleet hadn't seen her being hit. Even *Fiume*, directly astern of her, passed her by without her crew realizing she was in trouble. So, as the aircraft made their escape, and the firing eventually died down, Iachino's fleet continued on towards the north-west, and *Pola* was left behind.

Meanwhile, Saunt and his men had a new challenge to overcome. After the attack, they flew east towards *Formidable*. However, a signal from Captain Bisset ordered them not to return to the carrier, but to head to Maleme instead. That, though, was more than twice the distance away. Lieutenant Hopkins, in Saunt's Albacore, explained what followed: 'Not all of us succeeded in getting there, and, in fact, I believe only two or three of us, including myself, arrived at the airfield. The remainder ditched at various points around the shores of Crete, but all were picked up or got ashore.'

In fact, three Albacores fitted with long-range tanks all made it safely to Maleme, as did the two Swordfish from 815 NAS. Unknown to Hopkins, of the remaining five aircraft from *Formidable* only one (5A) was forced to ditch, and Sub-Lieutenant Williams and his two companions were recovered by the destroyer *Juno*. The remaining aircraft all managed to

The evening pursuit, 1945–2215hrs, 28 March

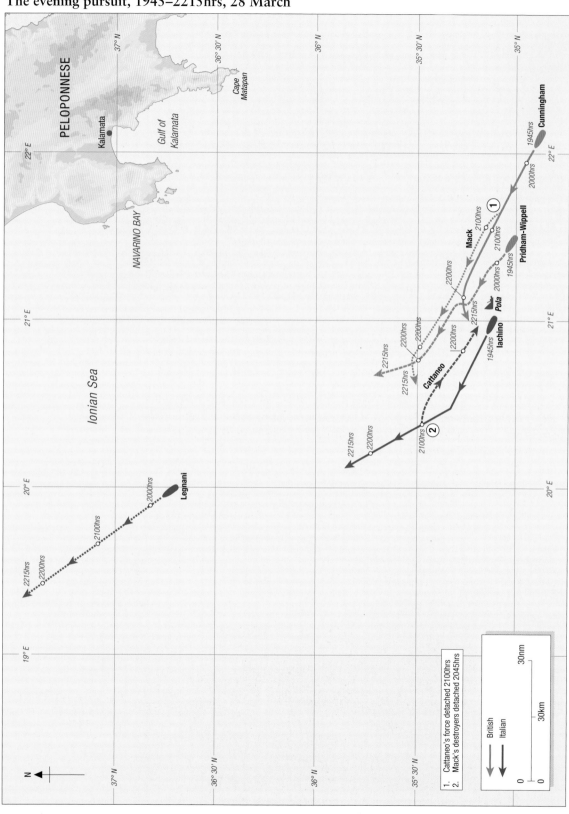

land near Suda Bay, to the east of Maleme. At 1950hrs Bolt, too, returned to Suda Bay, as a Swordfish from *Formidable* arrived to relieve him. This Swordfish, fitted with long-range tanks, would shadow Iachino's battle fleet throughout the night.

CATTANEO'S MISSION

The reason Captain Bisset diverted his strike aircraft to Crete was that on *Formidable*, together with the rest of the battle fleet, it was expected that a surface action was imminent. When Cunningham learned that the *Vittorio Veneto* had emerged from the dusk air strike unscathed, he decided to prepare for a night battle. This was an incredibly risky undertaking – one that flew in the face of established doctrine. Risking his three battleships and a carrier in a night action would normally have been considered foolhardy. However, the Mediterranean Fleet had trained hard for night actions, and he felt this gave him a significant edge over his Italian opponents. Also, *Valiant* carried an effective Radio Direction Finding (RDF) set, as radar was known by the Royal Navy at the time. This technology wasn't available to Iachino. Cunningham, then, decided to place his faith in his ships and men.

Meanwhile, after the last air strike, the Italian fleet resumed its old course and speed – 300° at 16 knots, and continued on through the night towards the Italian coast. A little after 2000hrs, Iachino received a report from the Supermarina headquarters in Rome. It told him that radio direction finders on the Italian coast had placed the British flagship 75 miles astern of him. Even then, Iachino was sure this referred to Pridham-Wippell's *Orion*, rather than Cunningham and his flagship. After all, no sighting report of the British battle fleet had reached him the previous day. In any case, that meant that he was now far enough away from the British that a night attack by enemy destroyers was now unlikely. So, Iachino decided to break up his fleet's tight formation, and separate the various forces again.

Cattaneo's cruisers were ordered to take up station 2½ miles ahead of the flagship, and Sansonetti's would deploy the same distance astern of the battleship. Each formation would be accompanied by four destroyers.

The Abruzzi-class light cruiser *Giuseppe Garibaldi*, sister ship of the namesake of her class, the *Luigi di Savoia Duca degli Abruzzi*. She formed part of Legnani's 8th Cruiser Division, which never came into contact with the enemy during the battle.

A close-up of the forward superstructure of Vice Admiral Pridham-Wippell's flagship, the Leander-class light cruiser *Orion*. In this picture the gunnery control tower is visible immediately forward of her foremast, while farther astern her Fairey Seafox floatplane is visible on its amidships catapult.

The remaining destroyers would form a protective screen around the *Vittorio Veneto*. It was then that the absence of the *Pola* was discovered. It was surprising this hadn't happened before, but the fleet had been sailing without lights showing, there was no moon, and Iachino had emphasized the need for radio silence. The news, though, immediately altered the whole situation. It was now clear that *Pola* had been damaged during the last air attack, and so had fallen astern of the rest of the fleet.

So, at 2018hrs, Iachino ordered Cattaneo's *Zara* to turn back with his remaining force to see where *Pola* was, and to assist her if that was practicable. Cattaneo felt this was risky, and suggested that he only sent two destroyers back to look for her. Iachino, though, was insistent. He wanted a senior officer on hand to assess the situation, and to make whatever decisions were required, even if that meant scuttling the *Pola*, or towing her into an Italian port. By sending Cattaneo back with his remaining force, he would also be better-placed to protect *Pola* in the event of an encounter with British light cruisers or destroyers. So, at 2038hrs, Iachino confirmed his order. At 2100hrs Cattaneo in *Zara* would reverse course, accompanied by the *Fiume* and his four attached destroyers.

As Cattaneo's force detached from the rest of the Italian fleet at 2100hrs, it formed up into a single column, with a destroyer leading, followed by *Zara*, *Fiume* and then the remaining three destroyers. By then Iachino had altered course again, and from 2048hrs the fleet was on a heading of 323°, which took it towards Cape Colonna, which marked the start of the Gulf of Taranto. They were also making 19 knots now, thanks to some makeshift repairs to the flagship's propulsion system. By dawn, then, they would be well within the range of Italian land-based aircraft. Without Iachino suspecting it, this increase in speed and change of course would also place the bulk of the Italian fleet beyond the reach of the pursuing British warships. Meanwhile, Cattaneo and his force were sailing headlong into danger. *Pola*, now some 50 miles from Iachino, would be the bait in a trap, even though none of the commanders at sea that night realized it yet.

Ninety minutes before, when the dusk air strike began, Pridham-Wippell in his flagship *Orion* was some 15 miles away to the east, just over the horizon. He had already sighted the Italian fleet, and by then he had dropped back slightly, awaiting orders from Cunningham. The crews of *Orion*, *Ajax*, *Gloucester* and *Perth* were able to watch the searchlights and exploding airbursts from just beyond the horizon. By the time the attack ended, night had fallen, and there was no clear sight where the enemy fleet was. So, Pridham-Wippell steered towards the spot where the air attack had taken place, hoping to regain contact with the enemy. With no moon and a haze obscuring the stars, it was a dark night, with visibility reduced to just four miles. At 2014hrs he ordered a course change to 310°, as he planned to keep a little to the east of the Italian fleet, rather than blunder into it in the dark.

A minute later, a contact was picked up on radar, some 6 miles ahead. He remained on his current course, though, and his radar plotters soon determined that the contact was stationary. Although nobody knew it at the time, this was the crippled *Pola*. Still, Pridham-Wippell maintained his course, making 15 knots to reduce the visibility of his cruisers' bow waves. His mission, after all, was to follow the Italian fleet. However, *Ajax* signalled

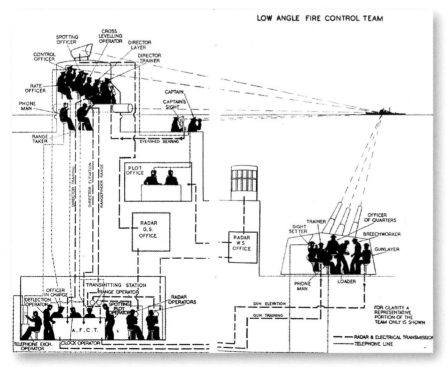

By 1941 gunnery fire control was well developed in both the Regia Marina and the Royal Navy. This shows the system used in a British Town-class cruiser like *Gloucester*, with information collated in the Director Control Tower being passed to the plotting room and the transmitting station, where firing solutions were passed on to the gun turrets. This also shows the integration of radar information, which at Matapan was only available to *Ajax* and *Valiant*.

the position of the mysterious contact to Cunningham. Over the next hour or so Pridham-Wippell continued his search for the enemy. Then, at 2145hrs, *Ajax* detected three unknown radar contacts, 5 miles to the south. In a rare moment of error, though, Pridham-Wippell mistakenly identified them as Captain Mack's destroyers, which were known to be nearby. Instead, it was Cattaneo's force, which therefore slipped past the British cruisers in the darkness.

The problem stemmed from Cunningham's decision at 2043hrs to unleash the 2nd and 14th Destroyer flotillas, under Captain Mack's command. These sped ahead of the British battle fleet, and by 2130hrs they had reached a point just a few miles to the south-east of the British cruisers. Pridham-Wippell knew that Cunningham had planned a night-time destroyer attack, and so when the radar contact was made by *Ajax*, he knew that his cruisers were expected to keep clear of the destroyers, in case they ruined the effectiveness of the suprise attack Mack was planning on Iachino's fleet. So, at 2202hrs, Pridham-Wippell turned away to the north. Meanwhile, Mack had learned of the radar sighting, and also assumed that *Ajax* had detected his own destroyers. He maintained his westerly course, and he, too, missed Cattaneo in the dark.

Worse, this turn to the north by Pridham-Wippell meant he was actually moving farther away from Iachino, rather than closer to him. However, at 2243hrs lookouts on both *Orion* and *Gloucester* spotted a red glow to the west. It was a flare, mistakenly fired from the *Vittorio Veneto*. Farther to the south, Mack had sighted it too. Even then, at that late stage of the pursuit, Pridham-Wippell had been handed another chance to regain contact with Iachino. By then, though, great gun flashes had been spotted piercing the darkness to the south-south-east. That could only mean that somewhere over there beyond the horizon, Cunningham's battle fleet had finally gone into action.

THE NIGHT ACTION

At 2043hrs, when Cunningham ordered Captain Mack to seek out the Italian fleet, his own battle fleet was left with an escort of just four destroyers. Then, at 2111hrs, *Warspite* received the signal from Pridham-Wippell reporting a radar contact with a stationary ship. The positon given in the message was just 25 miles to the west. So, Cunningham immediately turned to investigate. The battle fleet was now steering 280° in line astern, with *Warspite* in the lead, followed by *Valiant*, *Formidable* and *Barham*, all making 20 knots. The four destroyers were deployed ahead of the flagship, two off either bow. Visibility was poor, so they relied on *Valiant*'s Type 273 surface-search radar. At 2203hrs it detected the stopped ship 8 miles away, on a bearing of 244°. Cunningham turned the battle fleet 40° to port and continued with his ships in a quarter line, so each could fire her forward guns at the target.

By 2020hrs, when the range had dropped to 4½ miles, Cunningham ordered the destroyers *Greyhound* and *Griffin*, off his port bow, to move to the starboard side of the battle line, in case they got caught in the middle of a gunnery duel. They were on their way when, at 2223hrs, the destroyer *Stuart*, off *Warspite*'s starboard bow, spotted a ship 4 miles ahead of her, on a bearing of 250°. Soon, a line of darkened ships were seen from *Warspite* herself, passing from right to left ahead of them, at a range of just over

The night action 2215–0245hrs, 28/29 March

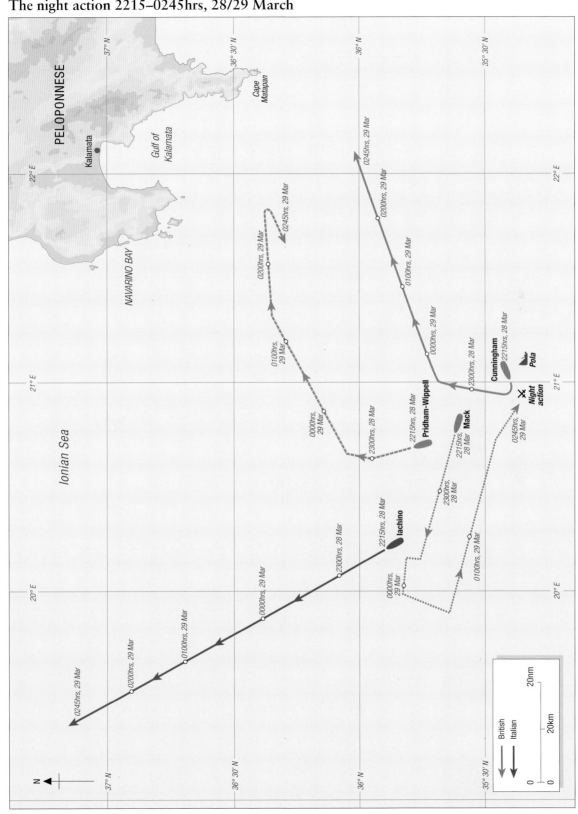

AMBUSHING CATTANEO'S CRUISERS, 2230HRS (PP. 76–77)

Thanks to radar, Admiral Cunningham's battle fleet detected the Italian cruisers at night, without being seen themselves. So, thanks to some deft manoevring, the admiral was able to place his battleships in a perfect position to ambush the enemy – now identified as two heavy cruisers, accompanied by several destroyers. Another stationary contact, probably a damaged cruiser, lay to the south-west. By 0225hrs the British battle fleet was in line ahead, steaming towards the west, on a reciprocal course to the enemy, who were now just two miles away to the south. The Italians had no idea what was about to be unleashed on them.

Then, at 2227hrs, on Cunningham's order, the destroyer *Greyhound* illuminated the enemy cruisers with her searchlight. Her beam illuminated the *Fiume* (**1**), the third ship in the Italian line, and the *Zara* ahead of her (**2**), as well as the leading ship, the

destroyer *Alfieri*. All of the guns on the unsuspecting Italian ships were trained fore and aft. Then Cunningham gave the order to open fire. Cunningham's flagship *Warspite* and *Valiant* astern of her opened fire simultaneously, targeting *Fiume* with their 15-inch guns. As the carrier *Formidable* hauled out of line to starboard, the battleship *Barham* (**3**) opened fire at the *Alfieri*. The battleships then opened up with their secondary 6-inch guns. Some of these 6-inch shells fell dangerously close to the destroyer *Griffin*. *Fiume*, though, was hit with almost every shell, and was soon a mass of flame; one of her after turrets was even blown over the side. Then, all three battleships shifted their fire to *Zara*, and she too was wrecked by five full broadsides in just two minutes. One of her forward turrets was blown into the air, and one of her boilers exploded in a pillar of fire. Within four minutes, the ambush was complete, and Cattaneo's cruisers had been reduced to burning hulks.

2 miles. They were steering a course of 130°, in a line-ahead formation. These were identified as a destroyer, followed by two cruisers, and then three more destroyers. It was Cattaneo. Cunningham reacted by turning his battle fleet back into a line-astern formation, with *Warspite* in the lead. Until then the 15-inch guns on the three battleships had been tracking the stopped *Pola*, which was lying to the south-east of the British ships. Now the big guns began tracking these new targets. At the same time, *Formidable* was ordered to turn to starboard, and haul out of the line towards the north. A gunnery duel was no place for an aircraft carrier.

On the bridge of the heavy cruiser *Zara*, Cattaneo had no idea that three enemy battleships were just 2 miles away, off his port beam. His flagship was preceded by the destroyer *Alfieri*, while astern of *Zara*, deployed in a neat line was her sister ship *Fiume*, followed by the destroyers *Gioberti*, *Carducci* and finally *Oriani*. All of the guns on the unsuspecting Italian warships were trained fore and aft. Then, at 2227hrs, on Cunningham's order, the destroyer *Greyhound* switched on her searchlight. She was a little way ahead of the British flagship, and just under 4,000 yards from the centre of the Italian line. Her beam illuminated the *Fiume*, and half of *Zara* ahead of her. Seconds later the three British battleships clicked on their searchlights, too. The leading four Italian ships were now bathed in light.

Then the battleships opened up with their main batteries of 15-inch guns. On *Valiant*'s searchlight platform was a Greek-born midshipman of royal blood – Prince Philip, husband of the late Queen Elizabeth II. Many years later, he described that moment:

> I turned my searchlight onto the bearing given by the RDF [radar] operator in the hope of seeing the target. Just then the destroyer *Greyhound* turned her searchlight on, which, I think, picked up an Italian destroyer, but the loom was enough for me to make out a ship on the horizon. I seem to remember that I reported that I had a ship in sight, and was ordered to 'open shutter'. The beam lit up a stationary cruiser, but we were so close by then that the beam only lit up half the ship. At that point all hell broke loose, as all our eight 15-inch guns, plus those of the flagship and *Barham*'s started firing at the stationary cruiser, which disappeared in an explosion and a cloud of smoke. I was then ordered to 'train left' and lit up another Italian cruiser,

This copy of a painting by John Hamilton shows the moment *Warspite* and *Valiant* opened fire on the Italian heavy cruiser *Fiume* during the first moments of the night action. In charge of the main searchlight on *Valiant*, shown in the foreground, was the late Prince Philip, Duke of Edinburgh.

THE NIGHT ACTION, 2220–2330HRS, 28 MARCH

After detecting the stopped cruiser *Pola* on radar, the British battle fleet closed to investigate it, guns at the ready. Suddenly, the Australian destroyer *Stuart* sighted a line of ships off her starboard bow. These were Vice Admiral Cattaneo's cruisers and destroyers, sent to rescue the *Pola*. Instead, they found themselves sailing into an ambush. Thanks to the radar fitted in *Valiant*, Admiral Cunningham was able to deploy his battle fleet so that it was in the perfect position for a gunnery action. When the destroyer *Greyhound* switched on her searchlights, she illuminated the Italian cruisers, and seconds later the British battleships opened fire. The surprise was complete; the guns on the Italian ships were still trained fore and aft when they were suddenly pounded by salvoes of 15-inch shells. After that, Cunningham sent in his destroyers to finish off the crippled enemy.

2220HRS

10

ITALIAN
1st Cruiser Division (Vice Admiral Cattaneo) – designated Force Z by British:
A. heavy cruiser *Zara* (flag)
B. heavy cruiser *Fiume*
C. heavy cruiser *Pola*
Accompanied by 9th Destroyer Flotilla:
D. destroyer *Alfieri*
E. destroyer *Carducci*
F. destroyer *Gioberti*
G. destroyer *Oriani*

9

2220HRS

6

1 ⚓

CATTANEO

B **2315HRS** **22**

35°20' N

17

8

▼ EVENTS

A

D **15**

2327HRS

2330HRS

1. At 2220hrs, *Valiant* detects a stationary radar contact to the south – the crippled *Pola*.

2. At 2223hrs, *Stuart* detects a line of enemy ships off her starboard beam, and raises the alarm.

3. Cunningham deploys his battle fleet into line ahead, behind *Warspite*. *Formidable* is detached, and turns away to the north.

4. *Griffin* and *Greyhound* are ordered to move to starboard beam of the fleet, to avoid them getting in the way of any gunnery exchange.

5. At 2227hrs, *Greyhound* switches on her searchlight, which illuminates the cruiser *Fiume*.

6. Other searchlights click on, illuminating the three leading Italian ships. The Italians are taken completely by surprise.

7. At 2228hrs, the British battle fleet opens fire, targeting *Fiume* and *Alfieri*, before switching fire to *Zara*.

8. All three Italian ships are crippled and set ablaze, then drift away to starboard.

9. The three Italian destroyers at the rear of the Italian line attempt to make their escape from the battle, and split up, with *Gioberti* turning south, and *Carducci* and *Oriani* east.

10. Cunningham orders the battle fleet to cease fire and turn away to the north, and instead orders his four destroyers to finish off the enemy. As *Greyhound* and *Griffin* pursue to the south-west, *Stuart* and *Havock* head towards the east.

11. *Stuart* and *Havock* come across *Zara* and *Alfieri*, and engage them with guns and torpedoes.

12. On spotting the *Carducci*, *Stuart* engages her with gunfire, while *Havock* launches a spread of torpedoes.

13. *Carducci* is hit by a torpedo, and sinks at 2315hrs.

14. *Stuart* spots the *Fiume*, while firing at the *Zara*.

15. The *Alfieri* sinks at 2330hrs.

16. *Stuart* sights the slightly damaged *Gioberti*, escaping towards the south. Farther to the east the *Oriani* has also escaped in the same direction.

17. *Fiume* sinks at around 1315hrs; the exact timing is unknown.

18. *Havock* spots the crippled *Pola*, stationary in the water; the destroyer turns away, as her crew thinks she is an Italian battleship. This report leads to the recall from west of the two destroyer flotillas to counter this imagined threat.

16

233(

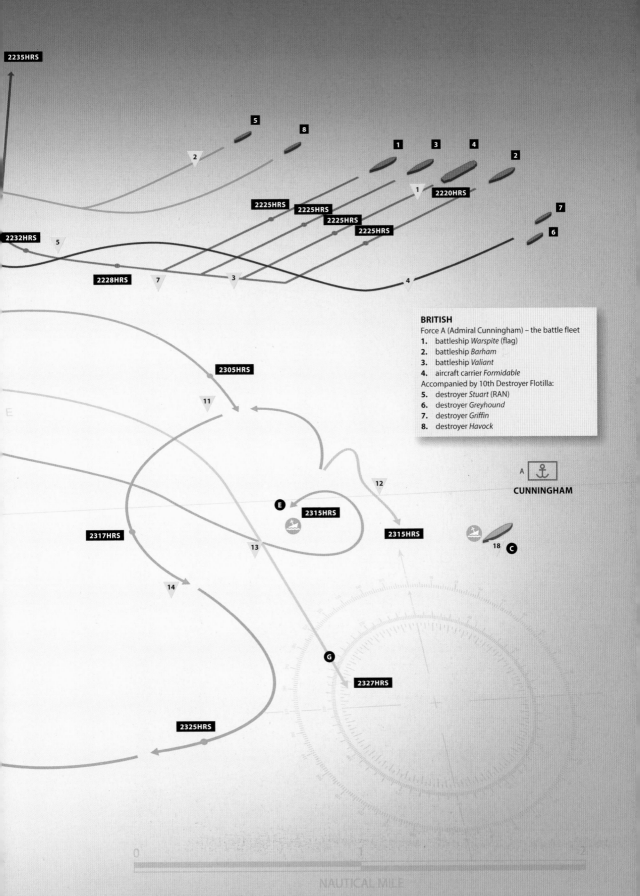

2235HRS

5

8

1   3   4   2

1   **2220HRS**

7

6

2225HRS   **2225HRS**   **2225HRS**   **2225HRS**

2232HRS   5

2228HRS   7   3   4

BRITISH
Force A (Admiral Cunningham) – the battle fleet
1. battleship *Warspite* (flag)
2. battleship *Barham*
3. battleship *Valiant*
4. aircraft carrier *Formidable*
Accompanied by 10th Destroyer Flotilla:
5. destroyer *Stuart* (RAN)
6. destroyer *Greyhound*
7. destroyer *Griffin*
8. destroyer *Havock*

E

A   ⚓
CUNNINGHAM

2305HRS

11

12

E
2315HRS

2315HRS

2317HRS

13   18   C

14

G
2327HRS

2325HRS

0   1   2

NAUTICAL MILE

which was given the same treatment. By this time the night was full of smoke, loud bangs and flashes, and the dark shapes of our destroyers, with their coloured recognition lights appeared and disappeared. That bit of the Mediterranean then became a very dangerous place.

Prince Philip captured the spirit of the action, but some of the details were less vividly remembered. The Italian ships were all steaming at 20 knots when they were 'ambushed' – the only stopped ship was the *Pola*, 5 miles away and out of sight in the darkness. *Greyhound*'s searchlight lit up the *Fiume*, and not a destroyer. The battleships opened fire at 2228hrs. *Warspite* targeted *Fiume*, at a range of 3,900 yards, on a bearing of 232°. Because of the angle, Y turret was unable to fire, due to the battleship's superstructure. Six seconds later all six shells hit their target, and the cruiser was turned into a flaming wreck. Holes were ripped in her hull and superstructure, and one of her after turrets was blown over the side. It was a death blow.

Valiant also targeted *Fiume*, firing at her with her four forward guns, before switching her fire to *Zara*. This time her second salvo, fired a minute later, was a full eight-gun broadside. At least five shells hit their still defenceless target, and the cruiser's B turret, just forward of the bridge, was blown into the air. Cattaneo's flagship was crippled, and was now ablaze from stem to stern. *Warspite* fired her second salvo at *Fiume*, hitting her at least six times, and leaving her a floating, blazing wreck, and listing heavily. *Warspite* then turned her guns on *Zara*, although by that time there was no real need. *Barham*, mistaking the *Alfieri* for a light cruiser, opened fire on her, and her first salvo set the destroyer ablaze. She hauled away to the south, trailing smoke and flame. *Barham* then turned her guns on *Zara*, which was pointed by her next broadside.

The destroyer *Griffin*, depicted moments after she first illuminated the cruiser *Fiume* with her searchlight. The Italian warship is already shown being torn apart by the British battle fleet, in this copy of a painting by maritime artist Jack Coggins.

So, in less that five minutes, two Italian cruisers and a destroyer had been put out of action. However, there were still three Italian destroyers left, and in a night action their torpedoes could act as a great leveller. At 2231hrs they turned towards the line of British battleships, and one

of them launched a spread of torpedoes. All three destroyers then turned away to starboard and tried to escape. The torpedoes all missed, but by now *Warspite*'s 6-inch secondary guns were firing at them, as were the British destroyers, and searchlights began illuminating the Italian boats as they turned away. In the confusion, *Warspite*'s 6-inch guns even fired on *Havock*, but fortunately the shells missed her. By 2238hrs it was all over. *Fiume* and *Zara* were burning fiercely, as was *Alfieri*, some way to the south-east. Cunningham ordered his main guns to cease fire. Instead, he would leave it to the destroyers to finish off Cattaneo's cruisers, and hunt down the fleeing enemy destroyers.

If the first part of the night action was calculated, clinical and decisive, what followed was the very opposite. It was so chaotic it was difficult to follow, and even those who took part had only a sketchy idea of what happened. Visibility had now dropped to less than 2 miles, and lingering smokescreens made conditions even worse. The job of pursuing and destroying the remnants of Cattaneo's force were given to the 10th Destroyer Flotilla, the only one left with the battle fleet. Its four destroyers were commanded by an Australian, Captain Waller RAN, who flew his flag in the Australian destroyer *Stuart*. When Cunningham's orders were received at 2241hrs, *Stuart*, *Greyhound*, *Griffin* and *Havock* were tucked away off *Warspite*'s starboard bow. Waller could see the three remaining Italian destroyers turn away to the south, to avoid the burning cruisers ahead of them.

A depiction (by artist Frank Norton) of the attack by Cunningham's destroyers on Cattaneo's damaged force, during the second stage of the night action. In the foreground the Australian destroyer *Stuart* is shown engaging an Italian cruiser.

The Oriani-class destroyer *Giosuè Carducci*, pictured leaving Taranto shortly before the outbreak of the war. She was hit by gunfire by *Stuart*, then torpedoed and sunk by *Havock* during the second phase of the night action.

Waller immediately ordered *Griffin* and *Greyhound* to give chase, leaving *Havock* to accompany *Stuart* as they stalked the Italian cruisers. The Italian destroyers made smoke as they turned away, which helped hide their next move. Essentially, they split up, with *Oriani* looping round to the north before turning east, racing past the British battleships. She even launched at least one torpedo, but it didn't hit anything. *Carducci* headed east, too, while *Gioberti* turned south. Waller turned to the east, parallel to the course taken by Cattaneo's ships before the ambush. At 2259hrs two burning ships were spotted through the gloom, and a minute later *Stuart* fired all of her torpedoes at them. The larger of the ships was hit, and Waller turned to the south-east so his two destroyers could fire their 4.7-inch guns at the enemy. Moments later, at 2306hrs, another explosion was seen on the larger target – now identified as the *Zara*, which was listing heavily and stopped in the water. Her burning companion was the destroyer *Alfieri*.

Suddenly, another Italian destroyer loomed out of the darkness, forcing Waller to turn to avoid a collision. It was the *Carducci*. *Stuart* managed to fire two broadsides into her before she disappeared to the east, pursued by Lieutenant Geoffrey Watkins in *Havock*. It was now 2308hrs, and *Stuart* was now left on her own, with no torpedoes left. Next, Waller spotted another cruiser to the south-west, and headed off to investigate. She was the *Fiume*, riding very low in the water. As the *Stuart* curved round to the south and west, *Havock* was heading to the south-east, in pursuit of the *Carducci*. After a few minutes, *Havock* overhauled her prey, and launched four torpedoes. *Carducci* was hit, and skewed to a halt, burning fiercely. She sank a few minutes later, at 2315hrs. A mile to the west, the *Alfieri* also sank at that point, her last moments seen from the *Stuart* as she sped by to the south of her.

At that point *Havock* became separated from *Stuart*, and coming across the damaged *Carducci* she fired a spread of four torpedoes at her. One of these hit the Italian destroyer at 2315hrs, and she slewed to a stop, blazing fiercely. She sank 15 minutes later. *Havock* then circled around, and catching sight of the burning *Zara* again she fired a four-torpedo spread at her, all of which missed. Meanwhile, Waller in *Stuart* had watched the *Alfieri* sink at 2315hrs, then steamed on past her, heading towards the north-east, to engage the two cruisers again. Five minutes later Waller spotted another Italian destroyer, the *Oriani*, half a mile to the east, but she disappeared towards the south before he could react.

Then, at 2225hrs, while heading west towards the *Fiume*, his lookouts spotted the *Gioberti* off their port beam, racing south. She was on fire – the result of an earlier hit by one of *Warspite*'s 6-inch guns. She, too, disappeared into the darkness. By then *Fiume* had vanished – she sank alone in the darkness at around 2315hrs. Many of her crew, though, had managed to abandon ship, and the spot where she sank was marked by a cluster of boats and life-rafts. For their part *Griffin* and *Greyhound* had fired at the three Italian destroyers as they scattered, but by 2320hrs they had lost sight of any enemy ships in the darkness and smoke. At that point Cunningham ordered them to retire towards the north-east, to rejoin the battle fleet.

After torpedoing the *Carducci*, Lieutenant Watkins turned *Havock* away to the south, and spotted a burning cruiser to the west – almost certainly the *Zara*. He launched his remaining four torpedoes at her, but they all missed their mark. *Havock* briefly fired at her, before Watkins looped around towards the north-east, in search of other targets. At 2345hrs he fired off a starshell, and in its loom he spotted another Italian warship – a large one. Watkins mistakenly identified her as a Littorio-class battleship, and turned away. In fact, he'd stumbled across the stationary *Pola*. At the time, Captain Mack and the other British destroyers were 50 miles away

The G/H-class destroyer *Griffin* shown here, together with her sister ships *Greyhound* and *Hardy*, and the Australian-manned Scott-class destroyer *Stuart*, were used to hunt down and destroy the remnants of Cattaneo's force towards the end of the Matapan night action.

The J-class destroyer *Jervis* was commanded by Captain Philip Mack, who led the Mediterranean Fleet's 14th Destroyer Flotilla. Like her sister *Janus*, she was armed with six 4.7-inch guns, and carried ten 21-inch torpedoes.

to the west-north-west, in pursuit of the remnants of Iachino's fleet. The message had Mack break away and turn towards the position given by *Havock*. Several minutes later, after a hurried consultation on *Havock's* bridge, Watkins amended his first signal, and now identified the enemy ship as a heavy cruiser.

That, though, came too late for Mack, as it was 0134hrs before this revised signal reached him. By then Iachino was too far away to catch – only Pridham-Wippell was near enough to intercept him, some 20 miles to the east of the enemy fleet. Cunningham had sent *Griffin* and *Greyhound* to investigate the mystery ship, and at 0140hrs they identified her as the drifting *Pola*. Many of her crew had already abandoned ship, and she was in no condition to offer any resistance. The senior of the two destroyer captains, Commander Walter Marshall-A'Deane of *Greyhound*, was uncertain how to deal with the problem, as simply torpedoing her would be inhumane. So, he led the destroyers closer, to help rescue survivors.

This was still under way when, at 0320hrs, Captain Mack's destroyer *Jervis* appeared from the west. He ordered the Italians to abandon ship, and at 0340hrs he fired a torpedo into *Pola*, which hit her. The cruiser began to sink, but she was still afloat 20 minutes later. Mack ordered the newly arrived destroyer *Nubian* to finish her off with a single torpedo at 0403hrs, and *Pola* finally sank. In fact, she was the second cruiser to be torpedoed by *Jervis* that night. At 0210hrs, as they approached the sight of the night action, Mack's eight destroyers began sighting survivors in the water. He detached destroyers to help, and then at 0229hrs his lookouts spotted the *Zara*, half a mile off his port bow. *Jervis* came abreast of the stricken cruiser, and Mack fired a spread of four torpedoes. Two of them hit her at 0230hrs, and *Zara* finally sank seven minutes later. *Jervis* stayed to pick up survivors before pressing on to help Marshall-A'Deane deal with the *Pola*.

By then all contact with Iachino's remaining fleet had been lost. At 2330hrs the closest British force to him was Pridham-Wippell with his four cruisers, about 40 miles to the east, and on a parallel course. Both Italian and British forces were heading through the night towards the Calabrian coast. *Gloucester*, at the end of the British line, had actually seen gun flashes through the darkness, on a bearing of 150°. That was the night action, being fought 35 miles away to the south. Then, in what was probably his only mistake of the battle, Cunningham sent a signal at 2312hrs which ordered all forces not engaged in sinking the enemy to retire north-east, to keep clear of the destroyer battle.

It was directed primarily at the ships of his own battle fleet. Pridham-Wippell assumed, though, as he wasn't in contact with Iachino, that this signal applied to him. So, at 2330hrs he turned his cruisers away to the north-east. That course took his ships in the direction of Cape Matapan on the southern tip of Greece. Unfortunately, it also ended any lingering chance of catching the remnants of Iachino's once-proud fleet. Cunningham's battle fleet headed in the same general direction, too, and shortly after dawn Pridham-Wippell would rejoin the battle fleet, some 50 miles to the south-west of Cape Matapan. That morning, search aircraft were sent up from both Greece and from *Formidable*, but the seas proved empty of the enemy. Where the night action had been fought, all that was left was a scattering of life-rafts. So, as Cunningham's fleet shaped a course back to Alexandria, all that remained was to send destroyers to pick up the survivors of a vanquished foe.

A twin 4.7-inch gun mounting, in this case one in a Tribal-class destroyer. In the four destroyers of Captain Waller's 10th Destroyer Flotilla, its Scott- and G/H-class destroyers carried the same guns, except in single mountings. These were the guns that fired at the Italian cruisers and destroyers during the closing stages of the night action.

AFTERMATH

At dawn on 29 March the remnants of the Italian fleet were roughly 110 miles to the south-east of Cape Colonna. Unaware that they had been pursued, Admiral Iachino had remained on the course that would take him back to Taranto, which he expected to reach at around 1600hrs that afternoon. It was perhaps fortunate, though, that dawn revealed empty seas. Although the nearest British naval force that morning was now 175 miles astern of him, the fear remained that he might be subjected to more air strikes. So, his exhausted crews remained at their stations. The coming of dawn had also revealed empty skies. The promised air support from the Regio Aeronautica never materialized, despite strident pleas that evening from the Supermarina in Rome.

To the north, the light cruisers *Garibaldi* and *Abruzzi* were well on their way to Brindisi, while farther to the south the destroyers *Oriani* and *Gioberti* were all that remained of Cattaneo's command. They, too, would eventually reach Taranto without incident that evening. Iachino had heard nothing from Cattaneo since late the previous evening. The suddenness of the ambush and the violence of the ensuing action meant that no report reached him until later that morning. Even the two destroyers were busily maintaining radio silence, until they were well out of range of their pursuers. Vice Admiral Cattaneo was killed in the first moments of the night action, and nobody else had the presence of mind to tell their commander-in-chief what was happening.

For their part, after its destroyers and aircraft searched for more Italian survivors, the British Mediterranean Fleet shaped a course for Alexandria, which it reached safely at 1730hrs on 30 March. The only incident during the return voyage came at 1530hrs on 29 March, when the fleet was attacked by 12 Ju 88s, operating from airfields in North Africa. The Germans were driven off with the loss of one bomber, and no damage was done, although two 250kg bombs narrowly missed *Formidable*. Early the following morning an Italian SM.79 which was shadowing the fleet was shot down by Fulmars from the British carrier. The fleet's safe arrival in Alexandria also meant that the Italian survivors on board now became prisoners of war. In all, 1,015 Italian seamen were rescued following the battle. The British destroyers would have searched longer, were it not for the very real threat of air attacks. Instead, word was sent to the Italians, and so the hospital ship *Gradisca* rescued another 160 men. That meant that 2,303 Italians were lost in the battle, most of whom were from the *Zara* and *Fiume*. British losses were limited to just three airmen – the crew of Albacore 5G.

The imact of the battle is a little harder to evaluate. At the time it was significant. While Cunningham was disappointed he hadn't caught and destroyed the *Vittorio Veneto*, the destruction of an Italian heavy cruiser division was a major blow to the Regia Marina. While the cruisers themselves were a significant loss, this didn't alter the naval balance of power in the Mediterranean. After all, the Mediterranean Fleet lost the heavy crusier *York* and the AA cruiser *Bonaventure* that same week, both through underwater attacks executed by the Italians. Losing three heavy cruisers in a single night though, together with two destroyers was a major blow to confidence within the Regia Marina. Despite British claims to the contrary, morale within the Italian fleet was still relatively high. It was more a case that doubts had crept in that the fleet's sleek, modern warships were not as effective as was hoped, without the equal commitment to both crew training and tactical ability.

As Admiral Iachino put it afterwards: 'The engagement had the consequence of limiting, for some time, our operational activities.' This was, he added, 'not for the serious morale effect of the losses, as the British believed, but because the operation revealed our inferiority in effective aero-naval cooperation and the backwardness of our night battle technology.' This, though, was only part of the problem. The Supermarina was paralysed by an aversion to risk, which in turn was the result of the attitude of Mussolini. Consequently, Iachino had been operating on extremely restrictive orders, particularly when it came to placing his flagship in harm's way. His decision to withdraw in the face of British surface probes and air

Italian survivors from Cattaneo's force, pictured in rafts the morning after the battle, from the Italian hospital ship *Gradisca*, which scoured the area of the night action for survivors, after being directed to the location by the British.

In both fleets at Matapan, the majority of the warships had open bridges. This had the advantage of offering the ship's captain a clear view almost all around him. This view, taken from the gunnery direction tower, is of the bridge of a Town-class cruiser similar to *Gloucester*.

attacks while off Gavdos was largely due to this pressure, rather than his own tactical judgement.

For Cunningham, the fact that Iachino's crippled flagship escaped was enough to tarnish what would otherwise be a perfect naval victory. This, though, in part can be laid at the door of the signal he sent after the night action, ordering unengaged forces to withdraw to the northeast. While this took his battle fleet away from any threat posed by the Italian destroyers, it also led to Pridham-Wippell breaking contact with the fleeing Italian fleet. This was not Cunningham's intention – he was merely concerned for the safety of *Formidable* above all, and secondly his three battleships. By then, thanks to a junior commanding officer and his bridge team misidentifying a cruiser as a battleship, Cunningham's best offensive weapon – his two destroyer flotillas – had already abandoned the pursuit of the enemy fleet.

What is significant is Iachino's comment about aero-naval cooperation. The failure of the Regia Aeronautica to provide him with reconnaissance aircraft during his sweep towards Crete placed his fleet at risk. So, too, did the air force's failure to provide him with adequate air cover the following morning. By contrast, Iachino was impressed by the air support afforded to Cunningham by *Formidable*. As he put it later: 'It is certain that the major successes of the day were achieved by the aircraft carrier, confirming the importance of the practical contribution which a unit of this type gives to wartime operations at sea, above all when the opponent is completely deprived of aerial protection.' It was true that *Formidable* and her aircraft played a pivotal role in the British victory. Despite her risible shortage of aircraft, she managed to launch three air strikes, which resulted in damage to two important Italian warships. If she had an ample complement of embarked aircraft, as the same carrier did later in the war, then these air strikes could have been considerably more effective.

Perhaps the most significant outcome of the Battle of Cape Matapan was that it gave Cunningham control of the Eastern Mediterranean, and with it reasonably secure sea communications with Malta. This control of the sea, though, proved to be temporary. In a matter of weeks Germany invaded Yugoslavia and Greece, and the British were forced to evacuate the Greek mainland. This debacle was followed soon afterwards by the Axis invasion and capture of Crete. These conquests were made possible, to a large extent, by the presence of a German Fliegerkorps – an armada of aircraft, who very quickly asserted their dominance over the Eastern Mediterranean. In the naval battle for Crete Cunningham lost a sizeable portion of his fleet, and the same seas off Matapan where he had defeated the Italian fleet were now effectively closed off to him.

Still, there was a longer-term benefit from Matapan. After the battle, the Italian battle fleet never ventured that far east again. Instead, it was left to Axis aircraft and submarines to harry the enemy in those waters. Despite British setbacks in Greece, Crete and even North Africa, the sea route between Malta and Alexandria remained relatively open. It would be the Beta Convoy operation at the end of the year before the Regio Marina was willing to make another sortie in strength. Even then, and for the remainder of the war, it resolutely avoided operating farther to the east than Cape Matapan. This, then, allowed the Mediterranean Fleet to play its part in fighting through convoys to Malta, and in laying the groundwork for the day in mid-1943 when the Allies would be able to strike directly at Mussolini's Italy.

The British fleet under way in the Mediterranean, during its return to Alexandria after the battle. In this photograph, taken from a Swordfish, a Fulmar can be seen flying an air patrol over the fleet. Below her the carrier *Formidable* can be made out, together with the three battleships of the battle fleet, while a destroyer flotilla passes them.

THE BATTLEFIELD TODAY

The Germans have a naval song, which states that 'no flowers bloom on a sailor's grave'. Similarly, with the Battle of Cape Matapan there is no neat and fully interpreted battlefield to visit, complete with a visitor centre, and there is no monument to the fallen, or to the victor. Today the sunlit waters of the Ionian Sea to the south of Cape Matapan are criss-crossed by important shipping lanes, between Italy, Greece, the Suez Canal and the Middle East. This is as true now as it was before war came to the Eastern Mediterranean in 1940. Of the places mentioned here only the ports survive, and a few of the airports. Even here they have changed significantly. For instance, Alexandria is no longer home to the British Mediterranean Fleet. The fleet itself no longer exists, nor the ships that once formed it. Taranto is still an important base for the modern Italian Navy, but even here the facilities are merely a shadow of those that existed in 1941.

As for the ships, they have all long gone, save for the wrecks, which are now war graves, and therefore off limits to sports divers. The *Fiume*, *Pola* and *Zara* still lie where they sank, close to the remains of the destroyers *Alfieri* and *Carducci*. They have all been rediscovered in recent years, and at least in the case of the cruisers these underwater remains have been examined and investigated.

For those of you who still want to step onto the deck of a wartime British cruiser or destroyer, then you can, by visiting HMS *Belfast* in the Pool of London opposite the Tower of London, a near sister of HMS *Gloucester*, which fired the Royal Navy's opening shots in the Battle of Cape Matapan. Similarly, HMS *Cavalier* in Chatham Historic Dockyard is an improved, more modern version of the destroyers that fought at Matapan; touring her can give a visitor a good idea of what conditions were like aboard these wartime destroyers.

As for museums, there is little available for the historian. The Italian Naval Museum in Venice contains displays relating to the wartime Regia Marina, but it lacks much that deals directly with the battle of March 1941. In the United Kingdom the Royal Naval Museum in Portsmouth, the Imperial War Museum in south London and the National Maritime Museum in Greenwich are all worth visiting for their relevant interpretive displays, ship models and collections of wartime photographs, ship plans and artwork. In front of the Imperial War Museum, too, are a pair of 15-inch guns – a direct link to the immense weapons which opened up on the Italian cruisers off Matapan that evening in late March 1941. The Fleet Air Arm Museum in Yeovilton, Somerset contains surviving aircraft of the type that flew from

Formidable during the battle, including a fully operational Swordfish. Its appearance at air shows remains a crowd pleaser. Also worth mentioning is the Italian Air Force Museum in Bracciano, Lazio and the Gianni Caproni Museum of Aeronautics (Museo dell'Aeronautica Gianni Caproni) in Trento, north-west Italy. Finally, the Battle for Crete and National Resistance Museum in Heraklion, opened in 1994, concentrates on the later land fighting on the island, but it also includes naval-related displays. Perhaps more usefully, many museums have audio recordings of survivors of the battle, which help give a better understanding of what it was like to fly in an Albacore, form part of a 15-inch gun crew or serve as a lookout on a wartime destroyer. Those recordings in the collection of the Imperial War Museum are particularly recommended.

The Italian fleet flagship *Vittorio Veneto* pictured on the day after the battle. The photograph, taken from an accompanying cruiser of Sansonetti's division, shows her down by the stern following the torpedo hit she suffered during the battle.

FURTHER READING

Brescia, Maurizio, *Mussolini's Navy: A Reference Guide to the Regia Marina 1930–45* (Seaforth Publishing: Barnsley, 2012)

Campbell, John, *Naval Weapons of World War Two* (Conway Maritime Press: London, 1985)

Friedman, Norman, *Naval Radar* (Harper Collins: London, 1981)

Friedman, Norman, *British Destroyers, from Earliest Days to the Second World War* (Seaforth Publishing: Barnsley, 2009)

Friedman, Norman, *British Cruisers: Two World Wars and After* (Seaforth Publishing: Barnsley, 2010)

Friedman, Norman, *Naval Firepower: Battleship Guns and Gunnery in the Dreadnought Era* (Seaforth Publishing: Barnsley, 2013)

Gardiner, Robert (ed.), *Conway's All the World's Fighting Ships, 1922–1946* (Conway Maritime Press: London, 1980)

Greene, Jack and Massignani, Alessandro, *The Naval War in the Mediterranean 1940–43* (Chatham Publishing: Rochester, 1998)

Grove, Eric, *Sea Battles in Close-Up*, 2 Vols. (Ian Allen Ltd: Shepperton, 1988–1993)

Harold, J.E. (ed.), *Dark Seas: The Battle of Matapan*, Britannia Naval Histories of World War II (University of Plymouth Press: Plymouth, 2012)

Heathcote, Tony, *The British Admirals of the Fleet 1734–1995* (Pen & Sword: Barnsley, 2002)

Lavery, Brian, *Churchill's Navy: The Ships, Men and Organisation 1939–45* (Conway Maritime Press: London, 2006)

Morris, Douglas, *Cruisers of the Royal and Commonwealth Navies* (Maritime Books: Liskeard, 1987)

O'Hara, Vincent, *Struggle for the Middle Sea: The Great Navies at War in the Mediterranean 1940–45* (Conway Maritime Press: London, 2009)

Pack, S.W.C, *Night Action off Matapan* (Ian Allen Ltd: Shepperton, 1972)

Preston, Anthony (ed.), *Jane's Fighting Ships of World War II* (Bracken Books: London, 1989; originally published by Jane's Publishing Company: London, 1947)

Roberts, John, *British Warships of the Second World War* (Seaforth Publishing: Barnsley, 2017)

Roskill, Stephen W., *The War at Sea*, History of the Second World War Series Vol. 1 (HM Stationery Office: London 1954)

Winton, John, *Cunningham: The Greatest Admiral since Nelson* (John Murray Ltd: London, 1998)

The Queen Elizabeth-class battleship *Warspite*, flagship of Admiral Cunningham, pictured after the Matapan operation while serving in the Indian Ocean. During the battle, almost as important as her main armament was her Swordfish floatplane, which kept Cunningham informed of Iachino's movements.

INDEX

Figures in **bold** refer to illustrations.